San Diego
Architecture
DOWNTOWN

**Highlights from the award
winning *San Diego Architecture***

Dirk Sutro, Author

Graphic Design,
Marc Hawkins, viadesign

Published by
San Diego Architectural Foundation
Thomas M. Anglewicz, AIA
President, San Diego Architectural Foundation

**San Diego Architectural Foundation
Guidebook Project**

Jack Carpenter, FAIA
Chairman, *San Diego Architecture Downtown*

Neil Larson, AIA, Photography Chair

Alison Whitelaw, FAIA; Gordon Carrier, AIA
Fund Raising Chairs

Robert Noble, AIA, Printing and
Publishing Chair

Diane Kane, historian and instructor,
and her students, NewSchool of Architecture
and Design

Kevin Carpenter, Assoc. AIA, Mapping Chair

Thomas M. Anglewicz, AIA
Randy Peterson, FAIA
Co-Chairmen, AIA San Diego Host Chapter,
AIA 2003 National Convention and Expo

American Institute of Architects,
San Diego Chapter
Jack Carpenter, FAIA
AIA San Diego, 2004 President

Library of Congress Control Number: 2003099127
ISBN 0-9726020-1-1
Printed and bound in the United States

SPONSORS

Titanium ($15,000)

Centre City Development Corporation

Platinum ($10,000)

Architects Delawie Wilkes Rodriugues Barker

Carrier Johnson Architects

Highland Partnership

HMC Architects

McGraw-Hill Construction

Reno Contracting

Gold ($5,000+)

Metropolitan Transportation Development Board

Architects Larson Carpenter

Bosa Development

Silver ($2,500)

Tucker Sadler Noble Castro

Mosher Drew Watson Ferguson

Bronze ($1,000)

Austin Veum Robbins Partners

Martinez + Cutri Corporation

Copper ($500)

Latham & Watkins LLP

Trilogy Real Estate Management, Inc.

Salerno Livingston

San Diego

I f you are among those who haven't been in
San Diego since "the war years," or whose
only impressions are what you read in the
national press—you are in for some surprises.
San Diego is not a "sleepy Navy town" anymore.
Several post-war booms have built a colorful
modern city with a uniquely regional flavor. Over the years our best
architects have quietly designed
some of the most interesting buildings anywhere, often overlooked by
the national media. In barely more
than a century, we've moved from
missions to Irving Gill's primal
modernism, to the Balboa Park-
inspired Spanish Romance Years,

Irving Gill

followed by decades of fine post-WW II modernism that began with Lloyd Ruocco. Most
recently, newer generations of architects—a mix of
San Diegans and outsiders—are re-shaping the
region, especially the downtown skyline.

San Diego hasn't had a complete architectural
guidebook since 1977. During the past 25 years
the entire region has come of age: its population
exceeds 3 million, plus another 1.3 million in
Tijuana. All told, the combined border population

Balboa Park

is expected to reach 5.7 million by 2010, 7.7 million by 2020. That constitutes a metropolis by any measure.

County Administration Building

Through decades of growth pains, this region has done more things right than wrong. Planners and architects come from all over the world to admire a downtown alive with a mix of new buildings and permanent residents, a beachfront that remains accessible, uncommercialized, and relatively uncrowded, and an urban park rivaled only by that other park in a place they call the Big Apple.

But you're Out West now. So. Go through this book about downtown San Diego page by page, front to back. Or flip through at random. Find whatever catches your eye. Get

202 Island Inn

out there for a look. Welcome, and we think you'll be impressed with this place we fell in love with a long time ago.

Horton Plaza

Major Milestones in
San Diego Architectural History

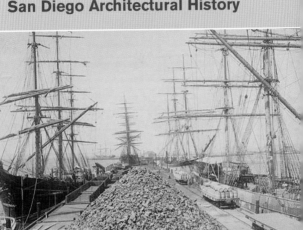

1769-1848	Mission Colonial Period 1769-1848
1867	Establishment of New Town
1915	Panama California Exposition
1917	World War I
1935	California Pacific International Exposition
1939-1945	World War II
1945- 1990	Growth of the Aerospace industry
1954	Establishment of University of San Diego
1964	University of California San Diego
1954-1964	United States International University and Expansion of San Diego State University
1961	Mission Valley Development
1964	Mission Bay Development
1975-present	Downtown Redevelopment-Horton Plaza, Marina District, Gaslamp, East Village/ Ballpark, Cortez Hill, and Little Italy

Using this guidebook

This book is geared toward anyone who wants to get out and see the best and most interesting architecture in urban San Diego. We've grouped projects by district or neighborhood, and provided some of each area's history. Each area has its own map. Wherever possible, we've clustered essential buildings within walking distance of each other, on one map. In many neighborhoods, you can park your car, pocket (or purse) this book, and explore architectural attractions on foot. By using the regional map, you can find mass transit to most destinations. Trolley lines and dozens of bus routes are run by San Diego's MTDB. If you travel by car, always consider car pooling. You'll have a clear conscience, and you'll take advantage of uncrowded car pool lanes on many San Diego freeways.

For more information on San Diego and our evolving downtown, contact Centre City Development Corp. (619-235-2200), or visit their downtown information center (225 Broadway, Suite 160).

For tourist information, contact the San Diego Convention and Visitors Bureau (619-236-1212).

Queries about architecture and buildings should be directed to the American Institute of Architects, San Diego chapter (619-232-0109).

For more information on San Diego's history, visit the San Diego Historical Society (619-232-6203) in Balboa Park.

The San Diego Architectural Foundation (publisher of this guidebook) is a tax-exempt non-profit California corporation whose mission is to encourage, inspire and challenge through education the development of excellent architecture in the San Diego region.

Contents

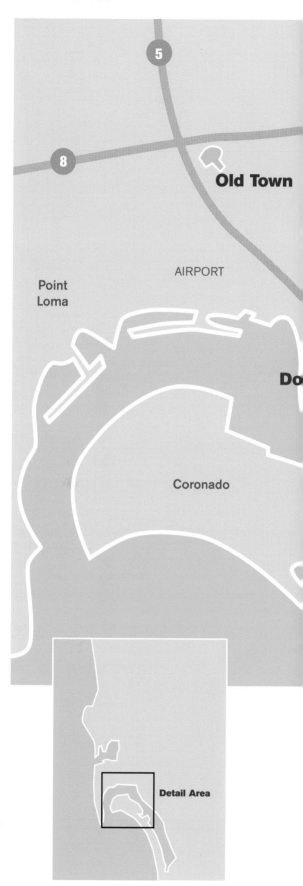

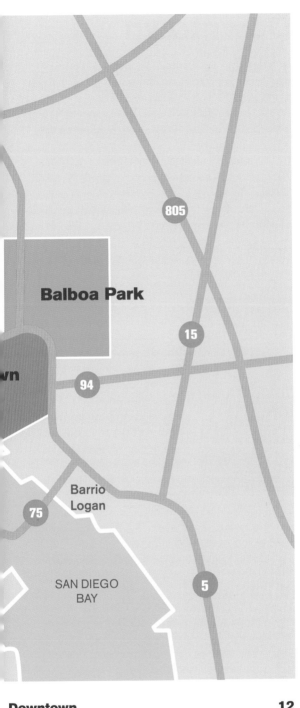

Downtown   **12**
   Core+Columbia   26
   Marina District   38
   Gaslamp   46
   East Village   62
   Cortez Hill   70
   Little Italy   78
Balboa Park   **90**
Old Town   **110**

Downtown

Downtown San Diego at the beginning of the 21st century is coming into its own. The skyline mixes stone-clad Chicago style buildings from the 1920s and 1930s with modern highrises ranging from flat-topped glass boxes from the 1960s to more recent designs with articulated tops. Known mid-century as a military town, the city altered its identity in the 1980s and 1990s. Aircraft carriers became less common and the Naval Training Center closed. Downtown was redeveloped with thousands of new housing units, thousands of square feet of new office space equipped for a new economy built on technology and communications, and public spaces and public art that provide breathing room in an increasingly dense urban center.

Launched in 1975, redevelopment downtown has been largely successful, scrutinized as exemplary by politicians, developers, and planners from other places. Created to spearhead this effort, Centre City Corp. (CCDC) has been a major force. Other cities envy the delicate blend of old and new: postmodern Horton Plaza next to Victorian Gaslamp Quarter, Mission Revival-style Santa Fe Depot sharing Broadway frontage with a Helmut Jahn high-rise, East Village warehouses next to new urban rowhomes. As an example of urban mass transit, the San Diego Trolley is another success story: soon after it opened in 1982, the red light-rail trains had higher ridership than predicted. They connect downtown with the border, Mission Valley, and East County.

A true urban neighborhood needs permanent residents. Thousands of new homes ranging from affordable rentals to luxurious high-rise condominiums have attracted a downtown population well on its way to redevelopment's target of 50,000 by 2020. Downtown residential developments designed by Rob Wellington Quigley, Jonathan Segal, and others have won international recognition.

The process of planning and approving the new Horton Plaza shopping center gave the first sign that San Diego would have high standards for its redevelopment effort. As originally conceived, the mall was a stock enclosed suburban scheme. But before it was approved, CCDC planners had prompted a radical re-design by architect Jon Jerde into a colorful postmodern place bisected diagonally by an multi-tiered open-air promenade modeled on narrow European streets. Jerde's design is much more suited to San Diego's character and climate. In the years since, the architect has become a celebrity for his design of high-profile projects in Las Vegas and Los Angeles, but San

Diego was the first city to take a risk on a new style of retailing that had never been tried before.

Along with Horton Plaza came new high-rise hotels, new office towers, a new waterfront convention center with an award-winning design by Canadian architect Arthur Erickson, and revitalization of the Gaslamp Quarter with public improvements and creative re-use of old buildings for new purposes—Italian eateries proved particularly popular. Public art and comfortable public space was also part of the redevelopment

Other cities envy the delicate blend of old and new: postmodern Horton Plaza next to Victorian Gaslamp Quarter, Mission Revival-style Santa Fe Depot sharing Broadway frontage with a Helmut Jahn high-rise, East Village warehouses next to new urban rowhomes.

agenda. In the early years several art pieces were proposed and rejected, but by 20th century's close, many thoughtful pieces had been installed, some of which reflect the region's multi-cultural identity. Perhaps most impressive in the realm of public art was the inclusion of art and artists in the process of creating the Martin Luther King, Jr. Promenade along Harbor Drive. This was an early attempt to make "art" more integral to the built environment, more than just a plopped down steel sculpture.

With the downtown core well on its way as an inviting place to live and work, redevelopment efforts expanded to adjacent neighborhoods during the 1990s. To the north of downtown, Little Italy became a vital mix of residential, retail, and commercial uses, while maintaining and building

on its ethnic history. East Village is destined to become downtown's civic showplace, with plans for a baseball park, a central library, and a new designation as Bandwidth Bay—a place for new buildings equipped with broadband and communications capabilities demanded by technology endeavors. Around the historic El Cortez Hotel, a downtown landmark restored as apartments, a dense residential neighborhood has developed.

Downtown's history began with visionaries such as Alonzo Horton. Before Horton staked his claim in the 1860s, San Diego's center was several miles to the north, in the area known as Old Town, the site of early settlement around the Presidio, and the original site of San Diego's Mission. Down the slope at the edge of the bay, East Coast traders loaded hides onto vessels for shipment back home around the tip of South America. Even then, San Diego was a diverse and wide-open place, a destination for dreamers. Juan Cabrillo sailed into San Diego Bay in 1542. Sixty years later Sebastian Vizcaino named the bay "San Diego". Richard Henry Dana stopped here in the 1830s, during the voyage he documented in his book *Two Years Before the Mast.*

"Everyone was anxious to get a view of the new place," he wrote. "A chain of high hills, beginning at the point (which was on our larboard hand, coming in), protected the harbor on the north and west, and ran off into the interior as far as the eye could reach. On the other sides, the land was low, and green, but without trees. The entrance is so narrow as to admit but one vessel at a time, the current swift, and the channel runs so near to a low stony point that the ship's sides appeared almost to touch it. There was no town in sight, but on the smooth sand beach abreast, and within a cable's length of which three vessels lay moored, were four large houses—built of rough boards and looking like the great barns in which ice is stored on the borders of the large ponds near Boston—with piles of hides standing round them, and men in red shirts and large straw hats walking in and out of the doors....

Early San Diego looking across the harbor to Point Loma, 1888.

"Our crew fell in with some who belonged to the other vessels and, sailorlike, steered for the first grogshop. This was a small mud building of only one room in which were liquors, dry and West India goods, shoes, bread, fruits, and everything which is vendible in California…. The first place we went to was the old ruinous presidio, which stands on a rising ground near the village, which it over-looks. It is built in the form of an open square, like all the other presidios, and was in a most ruinous state with the exception of one side, in which the commandant lived with his family…The small settlement lay directly below the fort, composed of about forty dark brown-looking huts, or houses, and two larger ones, plastered, which belonged to two of the *gente de razon.* This town is not more than half as large as Monterey or Santa Barbara, and has little or no business."

San Diego's center shifted to its current locale when William Heath Davis and Andrew Gray acquired 160 acres near the waterfront in 1850. They shipped lumber and prefabricated buildings from the East Coast. Remnants of their efforts remain today in the form of Pantoja Park on lower G Street—originally the plaza in what became known as "Davis's Folly".

In 1855, *San Diego Herald* columnist George Horatio Derby took stock of the evolving urb: "The three villages, then, which go to make up the great city of San Diego, are the 'Playa,' 'Old Town,' and 'New Town,' or 'Davis's Folly.'" At the "Playa" there are but few buildings at present, and these not remarkable for size or architectural beauty of design. A long, low, one-storied tenement, near the base of the hills, once occupied by rollicking Captain Magruder and the officers under his command, is now the place where Judge Witherby, like Matthew, patiently "sits at the receipt of customs."

When plans for a transcontinental railroad terminus in San Diego stalled, and epic winter rains in 1861 and 1862 were followed by a drought, Davis and Gray's develop-ment stalled. In 1867 Alonzo Horton bought 800 water-front acres downtown at 33 cents apiece, and two years later added 160 acres for $4,000. He laid out downtown's

grid pattern of streets, with his "Horton's Addition" centered first around Fifth Avenue, later along Broadway near the location marked today by Horton Plaza park and its Irving Gill-designed fountain. Without the alleys typical of other major cities, downtown San Diego as defined by Horton would later be ripe for large redevelopment projects covering whole city blocks.

Horton's real estate ventures boomed with a Gold Rush in Julian east of San Diego between 1870 and 1875. When the transcontinental railroad connected to National City in 1885, "San Diego became real estate mad," according to the Federal Writers' Project book
San Diego: A California City.
"People lived in tents on their lots until they could clear away brush and cactus. More frequently they sold out at fancy prices before they could settle on the land. Buyers bought from maps without inspecting the purchase, and in turn sold to other speculators sight unseen.

"Local people jumped on the bandwagon. Housewives, lawyers, clerks, ministers, maids and businessmen began buying and selling. Some speculators paid as much as $500 for a place in line to buy property. This became the first peak in a real estate rollercoaster ride that first delighted then devastated speculators on at least three occasions between the 1867 birth of the Horton Addition and 1906. Horton counted the greenbacks, then invested in more land or new ventures. He gave lots to the Methodists, Episcopalians, and Baptists for new churches. He donated land to people who pledged to build houses at once. He donated the site for the proposed courthouse. Sometimes he paid his employees with property." By 1869, Horton was grossing $600 to $1,000 per day. Horton House, a grand hotel, once occupied the site across from Horton Plaza now occupied by the U.S. Grant Hotel.

San Diego's military history was a prime contributor to the look and feel of downtown San Diego. The U.S. Navy's Broadway Complex at Pacific Highway is a lowrise supply

Parade passing Horton House.

depot and office building, in a spare, efficient style. Gigantic Navy vessels are the equivalent of moving horizontal buildings that slide by on the bay. Huge hangars once housed aircraft factories north of downtown, next to the airport. Marine helicopters land along Pacific Highway next to Spanish Colonial buildings—many military structures throughout San Diego were designed in the spirit of Balboa Park. The military hired Balboa Park architect Bertram Goodhue to plan and design projects including the Marine Corps Recruit Depot.

DOWNTOWN HIGHLIGHT

San Diego on the Wing

San Diego's aviation history is commonly thought to have started in 1927, when Ryan Aviation quickly built the *Spirit of St. Louis* for Charles Lindbergh so he could make the first non-stop flight across the Atlantic. But the region had been on the leading edge of aviation innovation long before Lindbergh's plane was built.

On May 21, 1908—his 30th birthday—Glenn Curtiss made his first flight in Hammondsport, New York. In 1911 he opened a flight school on North Island, for training Army and Navy pilots. But his prime inventions in San Diego were designs for amphibious airplanes as well as planes that could utilize the decks of Navy ships as runways. A Curtiss aircraft made the first successful take-off from a Navy carrier in 1910.

In 1911 at North Island, Curtiss made the first successful amphibious takeoff and landing in his Hydro. Curtiss built the first Navy plane—the Triad—and trained the first two Navy pilots. As a result, Curtiss Airplane and Motor Company boomed in San Diego during World War I (1914-1918). In 1919, Curtiss's NC-4 made the first successful flight across the Atlantic.

Curtiss was among the first to establish San Diego as a center of aviation innovation, and his efforts also helped attract the military as a mainstay of the local economy. He launched a string of milestone events that would extend through the 20th century, events that had a significant impact on the look and feel of the urban waterfront and its signature sights and sounds.

Through cycles of boom and bust, the military has been a force almost from the beginning. On July 29, 1846, marines went ashore from the 22-gun *Cyane,* anchored in the bay. *Cyane* was the newest member of America's small Pacific Squadron, charged with securing California's coast from Mexican forces. A small squad rowed ashore, met no opposition as they hiked up a dirt path to the Presidio, and raised the Navy flag "on a small rise overlooking the confluence of the San Diego River into the northern sweep of San Diego Bay".

By the 1890s, military vessels were homeported in San Diego Bay. Piers and waterfront buildings soon followed to serve them. By 1911, San Diego took control of its bayfront tidelands from the state, led by the lobbying of new San Diego Congressman William Kettner, an insurance broker. Bond issues of $1.4 million approved in 1912 and 1913 funded the purchase of 60 acres of bayfront land from Broadway to Date Street, as well as construction of Broadway Pier. Kettner soon found federal funding to dredge San Diego Bay so Navy ships could come through. The Naval Militia's 28th Street Armory opened in 1914, coinciding with World War I. Kettner lobbied San Diego past San Francisco and Los Angeles, and the armored cruiser *California* was renamed *U.S.S. San Diego.*

By 1919, the Navy had a shipyard at 32nd Street downtown, and by 1922 several dozen destroyers anchored at the foot of 32nd. San Diego's military identity was sealed in 1920 when the electorate voted to donate bayfront land and a hospital site in Balboa Park to the Navy. In June

Demolition of old Santa Fe Depot with new depot in background.

922, the Naval Supply Depot moved from Point Loma to
the Fleet Supply Warehouse by the Broadway Pier—where
the Navy's Broadway Complex is today. In 1924, the
Navy's first aircraft carrier, a behemoth crowned by a
broad landing strip, arrived in San Diego. For decades to
come, the grey bulk of carriers became as much a part of
downtown San Diego's identity as the buildings, and San
Diego was the nation's number one carrier port. Decades
before Goodyear blimps, the Naval airship *Shenandoah*—
buoyed by 150,000 cubic feet of helium—made her first
West Coast stop at North Island, where she was visible
from miles around. A predecessor of the Navy's airborne
Blue Angels flight squad—the Three Seahawks—was
assembled in San Diego in 1927 and flew over dedication
ceremonies at Lindbergh Field the following year. By the

mid-twenties, the Navy transferred its
submarine base from Los Angeles to
San Diego. Navy Pier downtown was
completed in 1929. Through these
years, military leaders were often con-
scientious about their industry's
impact on the form of the city.

"To its undying credit," writes historian
Bruce Linder, "the Navy realized early
that North Island would form an important vista from the San Diego bayfront
and unusual care was taken in building
design to ensure that the base (and thus the Navy) would
'blend into' the community. Key to this masterstroke was
the involvement of architect Bertram Goodhue with the
North Island designers." Goodhue's low, simple red tile-
roofed concrete buildings were good neighbors to
Coronado and to other cities ringing the bay—including
downtown San Diego.

By the 1930s, San Diego was the dominant West Coast
base for both Navy planes and their floating airports. Maj.
Reuben H. Fleet developed the Ranger flying boat, and in
1935 moved 400 of his Consolidated Aircraft employees
from Buffalo to San Diego. From its 275,000-square-foot
sawtooth-roofed plant next to Lindbergh Field,
Consolidated launched the region's first major industry. A
few years later, World War II sealed downtown's military
identity.

"A year ago San Diego was a quiet, slow-moving town,"
reported *Life* magazine in 1941. "But no longer. The
defense boom has hit it…changing the look of the town.
With the boom has come housing projects, trailer camps,
traffic snarls, bigger red light districts. But it isn't these
things so much that worry the old San Diegans. What
makes them fret is the change in the tempo of their town.
Until a year ago people walked leisurely down Broadway
or drove quietly through Balboa Park. Now they stride hur-
riedly, drive like mad. Nice old ladies a year ago sat on the
waterfront painting pictures of ships coming and going.

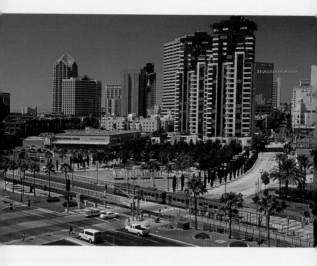

Now the ships coming and going are Army and Navy transports and nice old ladies are barred from the docks."

Conflicts in Korea and Vietnam added to the military presence in and around downtown San Diego. "Downsizing" followed in the 1990s, as the Naval Training Center west of Lindbergh Field was decommissioned. For better or worse, writes Linder in *San Diego's Navy,* "an unwritten partnership developed where city fathers generously traded protected anchorages and waterfront installations for protected economic growth and cultural stability…The Navy looked to ceremony and circumstance and played public relations spectacles to the hilt, nearly always well received by appreciative San Diegans." Today, in an era of military base closures, even though more than 100,000 military personnel are based in San Diego, it is difficult to imagine the spectacle of hundreds of sailors marching in formation up Broadway from the pier, past rows of Model A's parked diagonally in front of storefronts shaded by canvas awnings.

Because San Diego was a late bloomer and has never been a corporate headquarters city, the definition of "highrise" here is more liberal. Combine the lack of capital catalyst with an airport flight path that limits the height of downtown towers, and you get a skyline that reflects San Diego's modest place among American cities. One of Chicago's earliest tall buildings was Jenney's 7-story First Leiter Building in 1879, followed by higher neoclassical structures by architects including Burnham and Sullivan. San Diego's first tower in this spirit didn't come along until the Watts Robinson Building opened at Fifth Avenue and E Street in 1913. At 1,450 feet, Chicago's Sears Tower is three times as tall as any San Diego building. Landmark San Diego "towers" include waterfront Hyatt and Marriott Hotels, and America Plaza and Emerald Plaza on lower Broadway, none of which tops 500 feet.

William Templeton Johnson was San Diego's Louis Sullivan. Like the great Chicago architect, Johnson was a romantic in the Beaux Arts tradition of rusticated stone

DOWNTOWN HIGHLIGHT

Waterfront Plans

A stroke of political and planning diplomacy, the North Embarcadero Alliance Visionary Plan calls for preserving a mile-long stretch of downtown waterfront for pedestrian-friendly uses. Prepared by Sasaki Associates for a consortium of five public agencies (CCDC, city, port, Navy, county) in San Diego, the plan diverts auto traffic inland a block, from Harbor Drive to Pacific Highway. What remains will be a parklike "necklace of activities" between Broadway and Lindbergh Field.

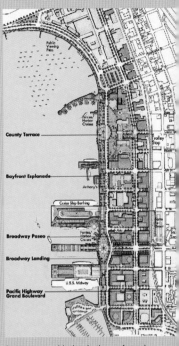

By breaking the area's long blocks into smaller blocks on a par with the rhythms of nearby downtown, the plan emphasizes visual and circulatory connections to the water, including views of Coronado Island and its sky-blue bridge. Central to the plan is a "bayfront esplanade" at water's edge, "animated by public art, urban scale street furnishings, public gathering places, scenic viewing areas, and a garland of pedestrian streetlights." Denser "civic precincts" would develop at Broadway (including a cruiseship terminal and two public piers—one of them probably housing the U.S.S. Midway aircraft carrier museum), and a few blocks to the north, where new public parks will surround the WPA-era County Administration Center. San Diego's successful opera company is lobbying for a Sydney-scale opera house near the foot of Broadway.

Implementation of the North Embarcadero plan, with $54 million in public improvements, will partially compensate San Diegans for what happened to the south, where a mammoth convention center and hotels limited visual and pedestrian access to a prime stretch of urban waterfront.

and classical arches and details. Johnson's 13-story San Diego Trust & Savings (1927) is downtown San Diego's finest tall building. Walker and Eisen's El Cortez Hotel (1926) is downtown's most visible tower, with its base of angled wings, square-shouldered shaft, and stepped-back top. In San Diego, there is no early tower as tall or inspiring as New York City's Chrysler Building, Boston's Custom House Tower (1915), or Seattle's 42-story Smith Tower (1914).

More recently, Frank L. Hope and Associates' Home Tower at 7th and Broadway (1962) was among the first modern steel-framed, glass-skinned high-rises—a dozen years after Mies van der Rohe's famous Lakeshore Drive apartments in Chicago. Among early bank towers, Tucker Sadler's First National Bank (later Union Bank) was most graceful and still looks good today. Deems Lewis & Partners' San Diego Financial Center (1974) was the first high-rise that hailed the beginning of redevelopment the following year. The 1980s brought reflective glass high-rises—many of them speculative endeavors that lacked the character of buildings designed for specific clients. The later part of that decade yielded more elegant towers such as First Interstate Plaza at Fifth Avenue and B Street—clad in red granite, with a spare plaza on the corner (due to siting, the plaza is usually in shade). Nineties high-rises by SOM (Hyatt Regency Hotel, Symphony Towers) and Helmut Jahn (America Plaza) are San Diego's best contemporary towers. The Hyatt on Harbor Drive suffers from a blockbuster parking structure. Trolley tracks pass through the base of America Plaza, activating public space between the tower and adjacent modern art museum.

Downtown San Diego has become a role model for redeveloping downtowns across the country. Much urban design credit goes to Max Schmidt, longtime head of urban planning at the Centre City Development Corp.—city government's redevelopment arm. Schmidt insisted on transforming the unsightly railroad easement along Harbor Drive into the imaginative Martin Luther King Promenade. A disciple of Jane Jacobs and William Whyte, Schmidt pushed for inviting public spaces, and was a constant critic of designs that weren't pedestrian-friendly. Schmidt was also instrumental in the transformation of Horton Plaza mall, from early enclosed suburban-style, to the colorful, open-air experience eventually designed by Jon Jerde.

In a new milllenium downtown San Diego is on the brink of two major new projects: an urban baseball park designed by New Mexican Antoine Predock with local architects, and a new central library designed by Rob Quigley. Both Predock and Quigley's designs draw from San Diego past architectural heritage. Predock and his collaborators have obviously taken a long look at the missions and the early 20th century modernism of San Diego architect Irving Gill. Quigley's design, with its signature dome, pays homage to Goodhue's Balboa Park, and to the dome of the old Balboa Theatre downtown.

While a portion of downtown waterfront was blocked off by the new convention center, there is good reason to hope that the North Embarcadero, between Seaport village and the airport, will make pedestrians a higher priority than commerce. Drafted by Sasaki Associates with a consortium of San Diego public agencies including the port and city, the North Embarcadero Alliance Visionary Plan diverts auto traffic a block inland, from Harbor Drive to Pacific Highway—freeing the bayfront for pedestrian-friendly plazas and paths. In the future, planners face many challenges downtown. They must find ways to accommodate and express San Diego's emerging technology-based economy. They must preserve historical buildings (many of which were already lost during redevelopment). They must push for imaginative new housing and high-rises. They must always keep pedestrians in mind as they find fresh transportation solutions to keep downtown San Diego from becoming a car-driven urban core plagued by gridlock.

Downtown Neighborhood.

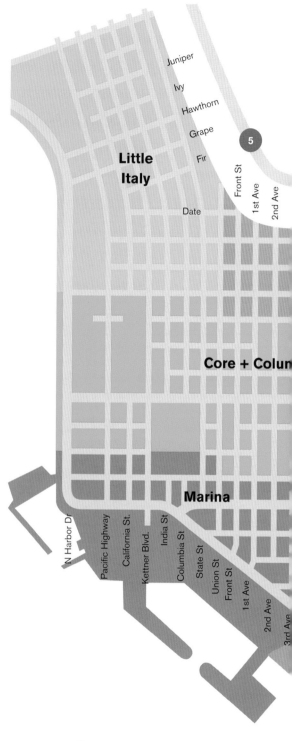

Juniper
Ivy
Hawthorn
Grape
Fir
Date

Little Italy

Front St
1st Ave
2nd Ave

5

Core + Colun

Marina

N Harbor D
Pacific Highway
California St.
Kettner Blvd.
India St
Columbia St
State St
Union St
Front St
1st Ave
2nd Ave
3rd Ave

Core + Columbia 26
Marina District 38
Gaslamp 46
East Village 62
Cortez Hill 70
Little Italy 78

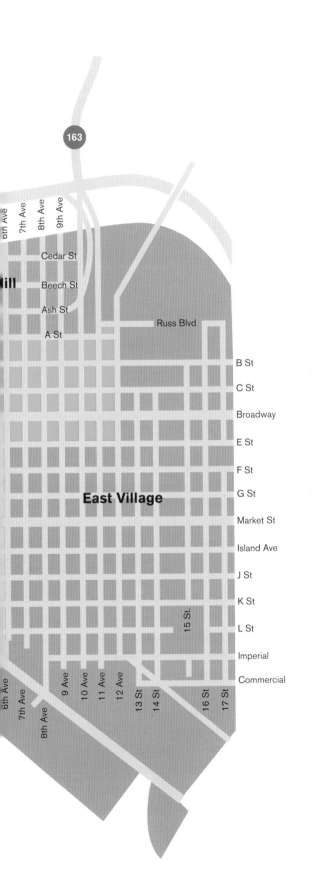

163

6th Ave
7th Ave
8th Ave
9th Ave

Cedar St

Beech St

ill

Ash St

Russ Blvd

A St

B St

C St

Broadway

E St

F St

East Village

G St

Market St

Island Ave

J St

K St

15 St.

L St

Imperial

Commercial

6th Ave
7th Ave
8th Ave
9 Ave
10 Ave
11 Ave
12 Ave
13 St
14 St
16 St
17 St

Core + Columbia Location

1 **Treo at Kettner**

2 **Santa Fe Depot Baggage Building**

3 **Santa Fe Depot**

4 **SDG&E Station B**

5 **America Plaza**

6 **Armed Services YMCA**

7 **Wyndham Emerald Plaza**

8 **Hall of Justice**

9 **Pickwick Hotel/Greyhound Bus Terminal**

10 **Spreckels Theatre**

11 **Federal Building (a) and U.S. Courthouse (b)**

12 **Horton Plaza Park and Fountain**

13 **U.S. Grant Hotel**

14 **Granger Building**

15 **On Broadway**

16 **First National Bank Building**

17 **San Diego Trust & Savings**

18 **Samuel I. Fox Building**

19 **John D. Spreckels Building**

20 **YWCA**

21 **Imperial Bank**

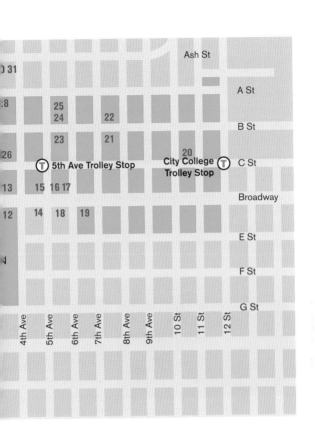

22 Symphony Towers

23 Union Bank

24 First National Bank Tower

25 San Diego Athletic Club/HBJ Building
World Trade Center

26 California Theatre

27 Security Pacific Plaza

28 Crabtree Building

29 Medical/Dental Building

30 Christian Science Church

31 SDG&E Substation C/
Consolidated Gas & Electric Company

+ COLUMBIA

1 / **Treo at Kettner** (2003)

1240 India & 1277 Kettner

CARRIER JOHNSON

One of San Diego's first new high-rises since the early 1990s, this full-block mixed-use project is a decent neighbor, with a stepped profile that preserves view corridors, and low-rise rowhomes that provide a pedestrian-scale streetwall and feature individual sidewalk entrances.

2 / **Santa Fe Depot Baggage Building**
(1915 & Planned Renovation)

1050 Kettner Blvd

BAKEWELL & BROWN
GLUCKMAN MAYNER WITH MILFORD WAYNE DONALDSON (RENOVATION)

Expanding its presence across Kettner from its building next to the downtown trolley station, the Museum of Contemporary Art San Diego plans to convert the former baggage building into three galleries and spaces for performance, film/video, and installation art. Gluckman is adding a three-story building of gray corrugated metal, with modern echoes of the historic depot's rhythms.

3 / **Santa Fe Depot** (1915)

1050 Kettner Blvd

BAKEWELL & BROWN

San Diego's signature Mission Revival building (it replaced the 1887 Victorian-style depot) was one of a string built by the railroad. Arched redwood beam-supported ceilings, bronze-and-glass chandeliers, oak benches, chromatic tiles, and Native American friezes hark back to an era of grand public buildings that resonate with California's history; the forecourt took advantage of San Diego's climate.

4 / **SDG&E Station B** (1911)

707 W. Broadway

EUGENE HOFFMAN & ANDREW ERVAST (ORIGINAL BOILER ROOM AND TURBINE ROOM)

WILLIAM TEMPLETON JOHNSON (1928 ADDITION AT NORTHEAST CORNER)

San Diego's cool steam plant, which once heated downtown's high-rises, is destined for redevelopment, perhaps as the base of a high-rise hotel and/or condominium tower.

5 / **One America Plaza** (1991)
600 W. Broadway
MURPHY/JAHN

This 34-story tower (sometimes compared to a Philips screwdriver) is a half-pint version of Jahn's 61-story One Liberty Place in Philadelphia; also an example of how hard it is for architects to design spectacular spires within the 400-foot limit imposed by San Diego's airport. At the street level, though, Jahn made urban design magic. A half-vault steel roof covers the s-shaped tracks of the San Diego Trolley station and its shops and restaurants. Across the tracks, a satellite branch of the Museum of Contemporary Art/San Diego adds a splash of activity, including public sculpture at the corner of Broadway and Kettner. Motion, art, public plaza, high-rise bayview offices, and pedestrian-friendly mixed-use—everything a prominent urban corner needs is here.

6 / **Armed Services YMCA** (1924)
500 W. Broadway
LINCOLN ROGERS/F.W. STEVENSON

The 260-room, Spanish Colonial revival and Italian Renaissance Y, which includes an indoor pool with beautiful tilework, was rehabbed as an SRO beginning in 2001.

7 / **Wyndham Emerald Plaza**
(originally Emerald-Shapery Center, 1991)
400-402 W. Broadway
C.W. KIM

This cluster of hexagonal spires is San Diego's most inventive high-rise. Developer Sandor Shapery's inspiration was nature's crystals. Architect C.W. Kim designed office towers up to 30 stories, an adjacent hotel to 28. Green reflective glass and a Donald Trumpish interior amount to sensory overload, but the sidewalk level is engaging, and this signature building looks great from a distance.

8 / **Hall of Justice** (1996)
330 W. Broadway
CARRIER JOHNSON

This new full-block home for the county's Superior Courts and administration utilizes sandstone walls, terrazzo floors, and blue-green glass to echo the primary San Diego elements of sun, sand, and water. A skybridge connects the new building to the earlier courthouse. The building is a bold new presence on lower Broadway.

CORE + COLUMBIA

9 / **Pickwick Hotel/Greyhound Bus Terminal** (1926)
132 & 120 W. Broadway
JAIME TOCHEY

Completed just before cars
became dominant transportation, this reinforced concrete
brick-faced building is ele-
gantly proportioned and
subtly detailed—note plaster
rosettes below the roofline.

10 / **Spreckels Theatre** (1912)
121 Broadway
HARRISON ALBRIGHT

When it opened Aug. 23, 1912, with George Broadhurst's "Bought and
Paid For," this 1,464-seat showplace was touted as the first modern playhouse west of the Mississippi. Albright created a space with no obstruct-
ing pillars or columns, a large stage for that era (82-by-58-feet), easy truck
access to both sides of the stage, and elaborate Baroque décor that
includes murals above the stage and on the ceiling (by Los Angeles artist
Emil Mazy), as well as classical statuary in wall niches. Don't miss a
chance to experience the tall, narrow interior, which places every seat
close to the stage.

11 / **Federal Building & U.S. Courthouse** (1976)
880–940 Front St.
HOPE & WHEELER

Completed in the
embryonic era of
downtown redevel-
opment, the rein-
forced concrete
courthouse gave
government a bold,
stark new image
with details that
include a skybridge and plazas featuring public art.

12 / **Horton Plaza Park and Fountain** (1871 & 1910)
Broadway between Third and Fourth Avenues

IRVING GILL (FOUNTAIN)

Mayors and public figures such as President Benjamin Harrison addressed San Diegans here from a bandstand that also hosted outdoor concerts. Flowing water and electric lights were an innovative and splashy combination when Gill dedicated his fountain on Oct. 15, 1910–the same evening the U.S. Grant Hotel opened across Broadway. Bronze plaques around the fountain's base honor Alonzo Horton, Father Junipero Serra (founder of Mission San Diego de Alcala), and explorer Juan Rodrigues Cabrillo. Horton Plaza Park was once downtown's prime public gathering spot, centrally located for shoppers and for bus and trolley riders. When it became a crashpad for homeless in the 1980s, lawns were replaced with shrubs, eliminating space for civic gatherings.

13 / **U.S. Grant Hotel** (1910)
326 Broadway

HARRISON ALBRIGHT

From his mansion on Cortez Hill (where the El Cortez Hotel is now), U.S. Grant, Jr., son of the 18th U.S. president, could monitor progress on the hotel he built and named in honor of his father. Merging old and new, the Neo-Classical hotel combines historical details outside and Queen Anne furnishings inside with then-modern techniques of concrete construction. FDR and Lindbergh are among celebs who slept here.

14 / **Granger Building** (1904)
964 Fifth Ave.

WILLIAM QUAYLE

Romanesque structure once housed businesses above ground, and zoo founder Dr. Harry Wegeforth's animals, in the basement. Original anchor tenant Merchants National Bank was succeeded in 1924 by Bank of Italy, and later, Bank of America. GASLAMP QUARTER HISTORIC STRUCTURE

COLUMBIA

15 / **On Broadway** (2003)

Broadway between Fourth and Fifth Avenues

BUNDY/THOMPSON

Re-using the Holzwasser/Walker Scott Building (1920/John Vawter) and the Owl Drug Building (1913/Quayle Brothers & Cressey), the new development includes 21 residential lofts, retail, restaurant, and commercial space. Walker Scott department store, converted now to a parking garage, was a centerpiece of mid-20th century downtown, known for its Spanish Colonial detailing and catchy window displays.

DOWNTOWN HIGHLIGHT

Horton Plaza

(1985)

Bounded by Broadway, G Street, First and Fourth Avenues

ARCHITECT:
JERDE PARTNERSHIP

Conceived as an open-air Euro-style shopping experience, architect Jon Jerde's Horton Plaza mall features a diagonal s-shaped promenade that slices through its center. An earlier design used the enclosed suburban format, but CCDC planners pushed for a re-design that takes advantage of San Diego's climate and

creates a strong sense of place at the city center. As a result, Horton Plaza became Jerde's prototypical shopping-as-entertainment project, one that set the stage for Universal CityWalk in Los Angeles, Fremont Street Experience in Las Vegas, and others. Between the multiplex cinema, food court, department stores, theaters, and boutique shops, you can spend an entire day here—a boon for Horton Plaza but a bane for adjacent businesses who wish the mall connected better with their streets. You may or may not like the sherbet colors, crazy signage, and eclectic historical references (columns, arches, domes, dentil moulding copied from the Knights of Pythias building, demolished during redevelopment), but there's no denying that a walk down any of this mall's serpentine sidewalks is an exhilirating mix of sights, sounds, food smells, and credit card eye candy—-an experience not unlike the compact European streetscapes that Horton Plaza emulates.

16 / **First National Bank Building** (1909)

NE corner Broadway and Fifth Avenue

FRANKLIN P. BURNHAM

San Diego's first high-rise offices, the 11-story Chicago-style building used an innovative reinforced concrete frame with concrete in-fill tile and truss rod supports. A penthouse was added in 1914; original decoration was stripped during a 1940 "modernization". The building was renovated by RTKL Architects to draw "technology-based" tenants in 2002/2003.

+ COLUMBIA

17 / **San Diego Trust & Savings** (1928)
530 Broadway
WILLIAM TEMPLETON JOHNSON

San Diego's stateliest 1920s building, designed in the Chicago spirit of Henry Hobson Richardson and Louis Sullivan— pioneering architects of high-rises distinguished by arches, stone, and delicate decoration such as the cherubs, flowers, leaves, and rosettes over the entry. The building was renovated and re-opened in 1999 as a Courtyard by Marriott Hotel.

18 / **Samuel I. Fox Building** (1929)
950 Sixth Avenue
WILLIAM TEMPLETON JOHNSON

A grand four-story showplace of reinforced concrete and steel that once housed Fox's Lion Clothing Co., the building features 16-foot ceilings, walnut window frames, sculptured terra cotta spandrels, and heraldic lion reliefs.

19 / **John D. Spreckels Building** (1927)
625 Broadway
PARKINSON & PARKINSON

Lancashire-born John Parkinson and his son Donald designed some of Southern California's most important buildings of the 1910s and 1920s—including Los Angeles City Hall and Bullocks Wilshire department store. Here, sugar millionaire John D. Spreckels' landmark structure in the heart of downtown echoes the Richardsonian Romanesque Revival style of San Diego Trust & Savings nearby, as well as architect H.H. Richardson's original early century buildings in Chicago.

20 / **YWCA** (1926)
1012 C Street
CLARENCE DECKER/F.W. STEVENSON

This five-story AIA award-winner (in 1933) has Spanish Colonial details including Churrigueresque reliefs surrounding entries; an indoor pool; and interior with Philippine mahogany ceilings and balustrades, decorative stone drinking fountains, tooled fireplace mantels.

21 / **Imperial Bank** (1982)

701 B Street

WARE & MALCOLM

San Diego's unflashy, 24-story "Darth Vader" looks better today than many of its mid-1980s peers.

22 / **Symphony Towers** (1989)

750 B Street

SKIDMORE, OWINGS & MERRILL

One of the best things about this building is hidden within: Symphony Hall, the former Fox Theatre restored in all its gilded glory. Outside, Skidmore Owings & Merrill did a graceful job combining a 34-story office tower and a 27-story hotel on this steep block, with the concert hall in between. Red granite exterior cladding upped the elegance ante in San Diego. Transparent glass at the street level connects interior and exterior space: pedestrians can see the 80-foot Deco-style oil-and-gold leaf lobby mural of an orchestra.

23 / **Union Bank** (1968)

525 B Street

LANGDON & WILSON

Another straightforward modern high-rise from downtown San Diego's first wave.

24 / **First National Bank Tower** (1966)

530 B Street

TUCKER SADLER & BENNETT

One of San Diego's first modern high-rises was also one of its best, with well-defined base, shaft, and top.

25 / **San Diego Athletic Club/HBJ Building/ World Trade Center** (1928)

1250 Sixth Avenue

WILLIAM WHEELER/F.W. STEVENSON/ I.E. LOVELESS

A 13-story Deco extravaganza, made of board-formed reinforced concrete. Ornate friezes and upper-level Gothic window details accent a mostly sleek modern building. Note the blue band of busts over Sixth Avenue—onetime members of the Athletic Club, perhaps?

CORE + COLUMBIA

26 / **California Theatre** (1927)
1122 Fourth Avenue
JOHN PAXTON PERRINE

Once promoted as "the cathedral of the motion picture," the nine-story reinforced concrete (i.e. quake-proof) Spanish Colonial revival building combined a theater with offices and shops. Parapets have red tile trim and dentils or arched corbeling. Plaster urns are among decorative details. The interior emulates a Spanish church. The Beatles' "A Hard Day's Night" played in this 2,200-seat venue, as did several rock bands. It was the last of West Coast Theaters' moviehouses designed by a regional architect— Pasadena's Perrine, the chain's most prolific architect.

27 / **Security Pacific Plaza** (1972)
1200 Third Avenue
TUCKER SADLER & BENNETT

More monolithic than Tucker Sadler's First National Bank Tower, this 19-story uses a zig-zag window pattern to stress its vertical thrust and bring natural light to offices.

28 / **Crabtree Building** (1962)
303 A Street
DEEMS-MARTIN & ASSOCIATES

A floating modern marvel of prestressed concrete slab floors cantilevered from four central columns, later victimized by renovation.

29 / **Medical/Dental Building** (1927)
233 A St.
FRANK STEVENSON

One of San Diego's early, elegant high-rises is this 14-story reinforced concrete structure, with granite cladding and interior marble. A fine example of its era's classical revival style, it exemplifies the notion among early high-rise designers that these buildings should have a clearly defined base, middle, and top.

30 / **Christian Science Church** (1904)
317 Ash Street
HEBBARD & GILL

Humble vine-covered brick building (formerly Goodbody's Mortuary, now occupied by attorneys) that shows Gill's fascination with landscape/architecture connections, with arched windows reminiscent of buildings by San Francisco Bay Area architect Bernard Maybeck.

31 / SDG&E Substation C/
Consolidated Gas & Electric Company (1923)
SW corner Fourth Avenue & Ash Street
REQUA & JACKSON

Combining the rich stone appearance of Chicago's H.H. Richardson and his Romanesque designs, with delicate Spanish Revival detailing, the building reminds us of a time when public utilities took pride in their buildings.

DOWNTOWN HIGHLIGHT

Coronado Bridge
(1969)

DESIGN CONSULTANT FOR THE BRIDGE:
ROBERT MOSHER, FAIA

ARCHITECT FOR THE TOLL PLAZA:
STEPHEN ALLEN, FAIA OF ANSHEN AND ALLEN

This 2.23-mile-long blue arc is San Diego's grandest piece of public art. The bridge employs the world's longest continuous orthotropic spans, utilizing a structural system, developed in Europe, which conceals struts and braces within a box girder to preserve the sleek, sinuous profile. The design of its supporting pylons was, according to architect Robert Mosher, inspired by the Laurel Street Bridge leading into Balboa Park, and makes a gesture to local history. The gradual arc of the roadbed maintains highway speed standards, and meets the Navy's clearance require-

ments for aircraft carriers at high tide. The color was chosen to blend the blue of the bay and the sky.

Marina Locations

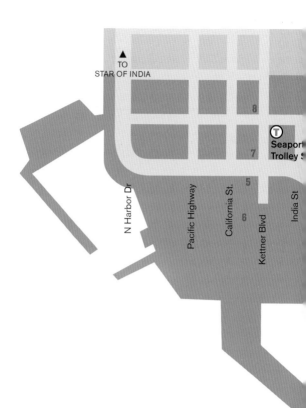

1 **San Diego Convention Center**

2 **San Diego Marriott Hotel**

3 **City Front Terrace**

4 **Hyatt Regency San Diego**

5 **San Diego Police Headquarters**

6 **Seaport Village**

7 **Park Place**

8 **Seven on Kettner**

9 **Pantoja Park**

10 **Metropolitan Correctional Center**

11 **U.S. Custom and Courthouse**

12 **The Meridian**

13 **City Walk**

14 **600 Front**

15 **Renaissance**

16 **Horizons**

17 **101 Market**

18 **235 on Market**

19 **202 Island Inn**

20 **J Street Inn**

21 **Pacific Terrace**

22 **Crown Bay**

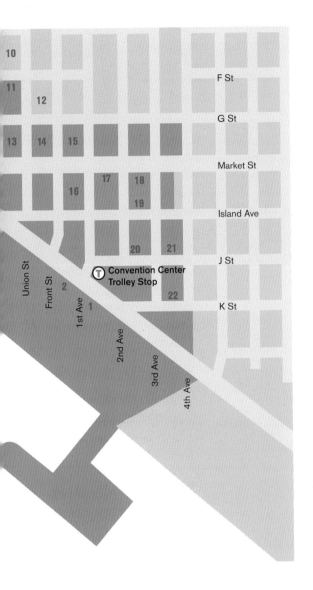

F St

G St

Market St

Island Ave

J St

K St

10

11

12

13 14 15

16 17 18

19

20 21

22

Union St

Front St

1st Ave

2nd Ave

3rd Ave

4th Ave

2

1

(T) Convention Center
Trolley Stop

MARINA DISTRICT

1 / **San Diego Convention Center** (1989 and 2002)
111 W. Harbor Drive
ARTHUR ERICKSON/DEEMS-LEWIS/LOSCHKY, MARQUARDT AND NESHOLM
(PHASE I)
TUCKER SADLER (PHASE II)

This 1.1-million-square-foot leviathan has
been a boon to the downtown economy.
From a pedestrian point of view it is impos-
ing, and it cuts off waterfront views and
access. But from automobiles, airplanes,
and boats on the bay it's an epic piece of
waterfront sculpture. Canadian architect Arthur Erickson's Phase I design, with
its flying buttresses, rooftop sails, and greenish skylight tubes, is visually poetic.

2 / **San Diego Marriott Hotel**
(1984, 1987)

333 W. Harbor Drive
F.L. HOPE (#1) AND WELTON BECKETT (#2)

These 25-story towers may look like twins,
but they are really only cousins. C.W. Kim's (at the time a staff designer
with Hope) original east tower cut a more graceful profile inspired by
spinnakers. The second, thicker tower accommodates more guest rooms—
but took the wind out of Kim's "twin sails" concept.

3 / **City Front Terrace** (1993)
500 W. Harbor Drive
SOLOMON CORDWELL & BUENZ

Chicago-style elegance came to San
Diego with this jumbo brick-and-limestone-
clad 13-story residential mid-rise, set in
Martin Luther King Promenade—the innovative linear park. One planning drawback:
the building's bulk casts a chilling afternoon shadow along Market Street
in a neighborhood where more modest residential redevelopment came
first. San Diego architect Milford Wayne Donaldson designed the renovation of the historic 4-story brick soap factory building here, as the loft portion of City Front Terrace.

4 / **Hyatt Regency San Diego** (1992)

One Market Place
SKIDMORE OWINGS & MERRILL

Skidmore Owings & Merrill is world-famous
for modern high-rises such as New York
City's Lever House (1952) and Chicago's
John Hancock Center (1970), but SOM's
more recent San Diego skyscrapers don't
embody that spare, singular vision. The
Hyatt's tapered top is one of downtown's
better crowns, but the street level's main
feature is a blockbuster parking garage that
belongs at a 1960s shopping mall—not
along a prime stretch of waterfront that
should be pedestrian-friendly. A second
tower was under construction in 2002.

5 / **San Diego Police Headquarters** (1939)
801 W. Market Street
QUAYLE BROTHERS & A.O. TREGANZA

In the Spanish Colonial tradition of towers, courtyards, tile roofs, and deepset arched openings, this romantic structure stood vacant for several years as preservationists battled development interests. As one of the few fine downtown buildings from its era, the headquarters could be put to new use and/or a portion preserved as part of some new project.

6 / **Seaport Village** (1980)
849 W. Harbor Drive
HOPE ARCHITECTS

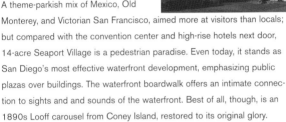

A theme-parkish mix of Mexico, Old Monterey, and Victorian San Francisco, aimed more at visitors than locals; but compared with the convention center and high-rise hotels next door, 14-acre Seaport Village is a pedestrian paradise. Even today, it stands as San Diego's most effective waterfront development, emphasizing public plazas over buildings. The waterfront boardwalk offers an intimate connection to sights and and sounds of the waterfront. Best of all, though, is an 1890s Looff carousel from Coney Island, restored to its original glory.

7 / **Park Place** (2002)
700 W. Harbor Drive
DIKEAKOS AND COTTER

Canadian architects add their 30-story impression of San Diego to the downtown skyline— bland, generic, with a swatch of tile roof that presumably adds a regional flavor.

8 / **Seven on Kettner** (1988)
702, 704, 706, 708, 710, 712 Kettner Boulevard
JONATHAN SEGAL

These New York-inspired rowhomes stand on an orphan wedge of land by the trolley tracks. Balconies, street-facing windows, and front stoops provide a Jane Jacobs/William Whyte sense of security. Segal's small-scale development set the stage for other small- and medium-size downtown housing projects that provide a richer fabric than old-school full-block redevelopment.

9 / **Pantoja Park** (1850)
G Street between India and Columbia

Originally the heart of William Heath Davis's 160-acre New Town, this area would have been a busy public plaza, but Davis's plan never panned out. In 1871, Alonzo Horton established a new central plaza on Broadway at Fourth Avenue. Today Pantoja Park is a public park next to condominiums built in the early 1980s.

MARINA DISTRICT

10 / **Metropolitan Correctional Center** (1975)

808 Union Street

TUCKER SADLER

Not often mentioned as one of downtown's land-mark buildings, this well-proportioned high-rise prison utilizes vertical strip windows to provide natural light while maintaining security.

11 / **U.S. Custom and Courthouse** (1913)

325 W. F Street

JAMES KNOX TAYLOR

Italian Renaissance reinforced concrete structure—which looks particularly striking when compared with some of the public buildings added downtown during the 1960s and 1970s.

12 / **The Meridian** (1985)

700 Front Street

MAXWELL STARKMAN

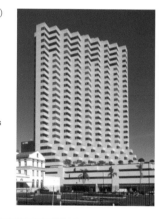

San Diego's first residential high-rise cuts a 24-story profile with its zig-zag view-grabbing southwest facade. A base of bulky horizontals looms over sidewalks like Fallingwater on steroids.

13 / **City Walk** (2002)

Bounded by State, G, Union, and Market Streets

MARTINEZ + CUTRI CORPORATION

Elegant street-level stone and imaginative Craftsman-inspired eaves are eye-grabbers, but the building lacks pedestrian-friendly details such as stoops—or, better yet, retail spaces. The mix of townhomes, condominiums, and lofts, plus the variety of forms and materials, equals a refreshingly rich collection of homes.

14 / **600 Front Street** (1988)

ROB WELLINGTON QUIGLEY

Mysterious clues let you make up your own story about this innovative apartment complex—a stairway-to-nowhere at the southeast corner. Unlike other low-rise urban apartments of this era, Quigley's is truly inspired by San Diego, with a central courtyard and outdoor corridors that take advantage of the weather. Quigley wanted ground floor retail to liven up sidewalks, but he was ahead of the downtown redevelopment curve.

15 / **Renaissance** (2002)

Bounded by First, Front, Market, and G

CARRIER JOHNSON

San Diego architects boldly abandon the faux-historical in favor of a sleek modern approach that makes its statement with large architectural volumes. Street-level retail grounds twin 22-story towers.

DOWNTOWN HIGHLIGHT

Martin Luther King Jr. Promenade

(1993)

Harbor Drive from Eighth Avenue to Broadway

PETER WALKER/MARTHA SCHWARTZ
WITH AUSTIN HANSEN FEHLMAN

Conceived by redevelopment urban planner Max Schmidt, this 1/4-mile linear park is a "serape" of colors, textures, water features, and public art in keeping with San Diego's cross-cultural heritage. The park is a pedestrian/bicycle/trolley thoroughfare connected to major projects such as CityFront Terrace and the Bridgeworks, with their adjacent plazas. The art includes bronze plaques bearing quotes from Dr. King; Roberto Salas's "Dream" near the Children's Museum; and

"Shedding the Cloak" by Jerry and Tama Dumlao and Mary Lynn Dominguez near Market and Columbia.

MARINA DISTRICT

16 / **Horizons** (2001)
510 First Avenue
ARC DESIGN INTERNATIONAL

Thoughtfully detailed mixed-use project that hailed a new generation of residential high-rises downtown. Ample, pedestrian-friendly first-floor retail space synergizes with 211 condominiums. An interior courtyard is an outdoor "living room" for residents.

17 / **101 Market Street** (2002)
101 Market Street Street
ROB WELLINGTON QUIGLEY

The Quigley firm refines the urban residential approach it pioneered in the 1980s: outdoor hallways, inviting corner entries, street-level commercial uses, thoughtfully concealed parking, and an interior courtyard that brings natural light into these homes.

18 / **235 on Market** (2001)
235 Market Street
WITHEE MALCOLM

Solid if somewhat generic low-rise condominium project that illustrates progress of CCDC planners in their push for articulated, pedestrian-friendly facades. Intense colors go a bit overboard—but beat the stock beige and tan of earlier redevelopment housing.

19 / **202 Island Inn** (1992)
202 Island Avenue
ROB WELLINGTON QUIGLEY

The architect's refined design for a "single-room occupancy" hotel (see his Baltic Inn) of stucco with aluminum windows, but at a larger scale and with concrete walls that reference parapets of California missions, well-disguised underground parking, a central courtyard for natural light (with a trickling water sculpture by landscape architects Spurlock-Poirier), and a cafe that animates this downtown corner. Raspberry and grape stucco sweeten interesting volumes along Second Street.

20 / **J Street Inn** (1990)
222 J Street
ROB WELLINGTON QUIGLEY

Smart angles and recesses that scoop natural light into rooms are hallmarks of another SRO ("single room occupancy") hotel designed by architect Rob Quigley. Fractured chromatic tiles and diagonal aluminum window frames energize the entry. Awnings add scale to facades and control summer sun, vertical slots in exterior walls admit natural light.

21 / **Pacific Terrace** (2003)
J Street between Third and Fourth Avenues
FEHLMAN LABARRE

Another new-millenium urban residential development that realizes many planning ideals: mixed-use (including street-level retail), intricately detailed facades, and imaginative (i.e. not all flat) rooflines.

22 / **Crown Bay** (2001)
350 K Street
WITHEE MALCOLM

A stylistic cousin of these architects' 235 On Market condominiums, this condo block's arches and vaulted roofs are stultifyingly familiar. The inclusion of ground-floor retail spaces marks a step in the right direction for creating a lively urban sidewalk scene that brings built-in security (William Whyte's "eyes on the street") to the downtown neighborhood.

DOWNTOWN HIGHLIGHT

Star of India
(1863)

1306 N. Harbor Dr.
Ramsey Shipyard,
Isle of Man.

A monument to San Diego's maritime heritage, this globe-traveling square-rigged tall ship—originally named *Euterpe*—was restored and resumed sailing for educational purposes in 1976.

Gaslamp Quarter

Downtown's first business and night life district spent roughly half a century as San Diego's prime place for lascivious adventures. Between 1885 and 1910, the city matured from a wild western town into an urban center. Between Market Street and Broadway, luxurious Gaslamp buildings such as the Backesto Block, Louis Bank of Commerce, Nesmith-Greeley, and Keating became centerpieces of San Diego's commercial core. Beginning with the Stingaree red light district of the 1870s, the southern end of the Gaslamp had a reputation; for several mid-century decades, into the 1970s, these 16 blocks flanking Fifth Avenue between Broadway and the Bay were known more for dive bars, X-rated moviehouses, and ladies of the night, than for legitimate businesses.

Architecturally, Victorian-era Gaslamp buildings were very much in keeping with the Queen Anne, Eastlake, and Italianate styles popular across America. Comstock & Trotsche, who also designed the Villa Montezuma, were responsible for the Gaslamp's Nesmith-Greeley and Grand Hotel buildings. Other important architects in the Gaslamp of the 1890s included Burkett & Osgood, John B. Stannard, Levi Goodrich, Charles Delaval, the Reid Brothers, and the Stewart Brothers. Merchants behind the Gaslamp's early growth were a multi-cultural mix: Asian-American, Mexican-American, African-American, Euro-American. The Chinese contribution is commemorated in the district by a small group of historic buildings.

Modernism came to the Gaslamp in the form of the Watts-Robinson Building (1911), one of downtown's first tall buildings, and the Golden West Hotel (1913), designed by Harrison Albright with an assist from Frank Lloyd Wright's son John Lloyd. As the business district shifted north toward Broadway, other "entrepreneurs" previously confined south of Market followed behind. Luckily the Quarter was spared from the variety of cold and uninviting structures built in San Diego and in many other American downtowns during the late 1950s and 1960s. In that era, new office space was built north of Broadway, while retailing shifted to Mission Valley and other outlying areas.

In 1974, with the assistance of the city, gaslamp merchants and property owners began dusting off and reviving their neighborhood as a destination for mainstream San Diegans. Following a survey of buildings by historian Ray Brandes, with the initiative of city planner Michael J. Stepner, the entire district received National Register of Historic Places status in 1980, triggering tax incentives that helped restore centerpiece buildings.

Sidewalks were widened and paved with brick, street trees and period street lamps were added. Porno palaces and liquor stores catering to transients were squeezed out. The opening of the San Diego Trolley along Harbor Drive lined with new high-rise hotels and condominiums and a new waterfront Convention Center brought a new concentration of residents and visitors to the the Gaslamp southern end, feeding the revitalization.

Skeptics predicted the opening of the nearby Horton Plaza mall in 1984 might take away the Gaslamp's momentum, but the district made the most of its gorgeous Queen Anne buildings, many of which were adapted for use as restaurants, fashion boutiques, live-work lofts, night clubs, and upscale shops aimed at both locals and tourists. With few exceptions, planners and architects maintained scale and historic character as new projects such as Bridgeworks (re-designed several times), a multiplex cinema, and tasteful small office buildings were added. Even the new Park-It-On-Market structure just east of the Quarter has architectural character.

By the beginning of the 21st century, the Gaslamp Quarter had become downtown San Diego's most magnetic neighborhood. All day and into the night, conventioneers, tourists, and locals take in the sights and sounds on foot—the Gaslamp has become a pedestrian-friendly entertainment and shopping mecca rivaled locally only by downtown La Jolla. Downtown's original urban center, now adapting to its third century, has become a model for mixing preservation with new development.

Gaslamp Locations

1 Lawyer's Block Building

2 Balboa Theatre

3 Ingle Building/Golden Lion

4 Horton on Fourth Apartments

5 Golden West Hotel

6 Lester Hotel

7 Royal Pie Bakery

8 Horton Grand/Kahle Saddlery Hotels

9 Grand Pacific Hotel

10 Pioneer Warehouse Lofts

11 Bridgeworks

12 Gaslamp Quarter Park

13 Brunswig Drug Company

14 East West Building

15 William Heath Davis House

16 Wimmer-Yamada Building

17 The Baltic Inn

18 Backesto Building

19 McGurck Building/Z Gallerie

20 I.O.O.F. Building

21 Yuma Building

22 Aztec Theatre/Urban Outfitters

23 Old City Hall

24 Cole Block Building

25 Gaslamp Pacific Stadium 15

26 Llewelyn Building

27 Loring Building/Fritz Building

28 Spencer Ogden/DeLaval Building

29 George Hill Building

30 St. James Hotel

31 Marston Building

32 Nesmith-Greeley Building

33 Louis Bank of Commerce

34 Keating Building

35 Ingersoll Tutton Building

36 San Diego Hardware

37 Onyx Building

38 Watts-Robinson Building/
Jewelers Exchange

39 Dalton Building

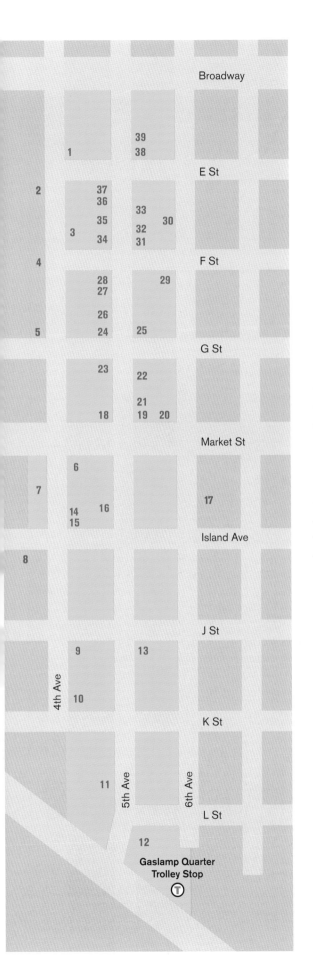

Broadway

39
38

1

E St

2

37
36
35
34
3

33
32
31
30

4

F St

28
27
26
24
5

29

25

G St

23
18

22
21
19 20

Market St

6
7
14
15
16

17

Island Ave

8

J St

9
10
13

4th Ave

K St

11
5th Ave
6th Ave

L St

12

**Gaslamp Quarter
Trolley Stop**
Ⓣ

GASLAMP QUARTER

1 / **Lawyer's Block Building** (1889)
919 Fourth Ave.
MCDOUGALL AND SONS

Longtime home to San Diego barristers, this structure mixes Italian Renaissance and Victorian details with Roman arches and pilasters.

GASLAMP QUARTER HISTORIC STRUCTURE

2 / **Balboa Theatre** (1924)
Fourth and E St.
WILLIAM WHEELER

Downtown's landmark theater had been mostly dormant since the mid-1980s, until renewed renovation efforts began in 2001. This 1,500-seat playhouse showcased both movies and stage dramas, with its sizeable orchestra pit, stage, and overhead "fly space" for scenery. Waterfalls flanking the stage gushed during intermissions. The tiled dome is a cousin of domes on the Santa Fe Depot downtown, and on the California Tower in Balboa Park. Visionary planners included the Balboa in the Horton Plaza mall redevelopment scheme.

GASLAMP QUARTER HISTORIC STRUCTURE

3 / **Ingle Building/Golden Lion** (1906)
424 F St.
EDWARD QUAYLE

A prototypical renovation that hailed the beginning of the Gaslamp's rebirth in 1982, this building had its stained glass windows restored, and a 25-foot stained-glass dome from the Stockton Elks Club, circa 1906, was added, along with the mural along F Street.

4 / **Horton on Fourth Apartments** (1994)
808 Fourth Ave.
CARRIER JOHNSON

After a decade of look-
ing at the exposed steel-
and-concrete edge of
Horton Plaza's parking
structure, this inventive
project filled the long
narrow strip between the garage and the sidewalk with 66 residential
units above street-level restaurant and retail spaces. The architecture combines modern details and uptempo colors with a scale that suits the
neighborhood.

5 / **Golden West Hotel** (1913)
720 Fourth Ave.
HARRISON ALBRIGHT WITH JOHN LLOYD WRIGHT

Frank Lloyd Wright
designed unbuilt proj-
ects for San Diego;
his son John realized
a handful of designs
here. He collaborated
on the Golden West as a 19-year-old in the office of San Diego architect
Harrison Albright. Originally a blue collar hotel, this reinforced concrete
block structure features corner sculptures by Alfonzo Ianelli, hired in 1914
by FLW to create sculpture for Midway Gardens in Chicago.

GASLAMP QUARTER HISTORIC STRUCTURE

6 / **Lester Hotel** (1906)
417 Market St.
WILLIAM QUAYLE

A cornerstone of early San Diego
night life, this building housed the
Goodwill Bar from 1906 to
1945, a pool hall beginning in
1923, and downtown's famed McDini's Corned Beef beginning in 1945.
The Lester Hotel opened here in 1915. Note the decorative brick at the
roofline and the diagonal corner entry. GASLAMP QUARTER HISTORIC STRUCTURE

7 / **Royal Pie Bakery** (1884)
554, 558, 560 Fourth Ave.

In the early 1980s, you could
still smell sweet potato pies
baking here, before the space
became an Irish pub. Upstairs,
the Anchor Hotel was a turn-
of-the-century favorite spot for
hookers and their clients; citing
"rampant immorality," building
owner Martha Kuhnel closed the hotel in the 1920s. Now occupied by
contemporary restaurants.

GASLAMP QUARTER

8 / **Horton Grand/Kahle Saddlery Hotels**
(1886-8/1980s)

311 Island Ave.

M.W. DONALDSON
(RECONSTRUCTION)

San Diego's oldest Victorian
hotel, the Grand was renamed
the Hotel Horton in 1907. In
1981 the Horton and the downtown Kahle Saddlery were taken apart
and re-assembled here as a single hotel joined by a new atrium, with the
Horton on the left and the Saddlery on the right.

GASLAMP QUARTER HISTORIC STRUCTURE

9 / **Grand Pacific Hotel** (1887)
437 J St.

CLEMENT & STANNARD

The Gaslamp's only Victorian
hotel still in its original location,
the Grand Pacific was home to
Children's Hospital and various
children's agencies. Brick veneer
facings, iron cornices and columns, and plate-glass windows make this
one of the most distinctive Victorian-style buildings in the Gaslamp.

GASLAMP QUARTER HISTORIC STRUCTURE

10 / **Pioneer Warehouse Lofts** (1919/1991)
311 Fourth Ave.

EUGENE HOFFMAN

A smart conversion (by Bundy &
Thompson) of a cast concrete
and brick warehouse building
into 85 live-work lofts paved the
way for many other adaptations
of nearby period buildings for
contemporary uses.

11 / **Bridgeworks** (2000)
Fifth Avenue between K Street and Harbor Drive

CARRIER JOHNSON

Originally presented as a blockbuster project including a highrise tower
that would have dwarfed adjacent historical buildings, Bridgeworks is the
positive result of several years of haggling between the developer, architect, and city planners. A reduced hotel tower was built behind a lowrise
retail strip that
suits the scale of
Fifth Avenue and
incorporates bricks
and design details
from the T.M.
Cobb warehouse
that formerly stood
here.

Asian-Pacific Historic District

Since the turn of the 20th century, Chinese-Americans have been a force in the Gaslamp Quarter. Recognition of their impact came with the creation in 1987 of this Gaslamp adjunct district, bounded by Second, Sixth, Market, and J streets, and

including more than a dozen historic structures. Some of the architecture exhibits Asian roots. Buildings here include: Chinese Laundry (1923), 527 Fourth Ave, occupied most recently by an art gallery; Casa de Tomas Addition/Sewing Factory (1930), 520 Fourth Ave.; Tai Sing building (1923), 539 Fourth Ave; Quin Building (1930), 500 Fourth Ave.; the red-tile-roofed Lincoln Hotel (1913), 536 Fifth Ave.; and the Pacifica Hotel (1910), 547 Fourth Ave., once a Chinese-owned warehouse, a dance hall, and, most recently, a restaurant with a flamenco club in the basement. Also note the Manila Cafe (1930), 515 Fifth Avenue, where former San Diego Mayor Maureen O'Connor's father, once a popular local boxer known as Kid O'Connor, ran a billiard hall on the ground floor from 1939 to 1943; the Nanking Cafe (1912), 467 Fifth Ave., with details including a cast-iron column decorated with 3/4-inch tiles; the Chinese Mission Building (1927), 400 Third Avenue–designed by Irving Gill's nephew Louis Gill–one of the Gaslamp's few Mission Revival style, featuring a clay tile roof and bell tower; the Chinese Consolidated Benevolent Association (1911), 428 Third Avenue, where original tenants the Gee Goon Tong helped plot the 1912 revolution that made China a republic; and the Ying-On Merchants & Labor Benevolent Association (1925), 500 3rd Avenue.

12 / **Gaslamp Quarter Park** (1994)

Foot of Fifth Avenue

In Martin Luther King Promenade, by trolley tracks

AUSTIN HANSEN DESIGN GROUP

A fountain of unpredictable water spouts designed by L.A.'s Wet Design makes this Parterre-designed plaza an entertaining place for tourists and locals, children and adults who still know fun when they see it.

GASLAMP QUARTER

13 / **Brunswig Drug Company** (1900)
363 Fifth Ave.

This brick building, with its cast-iron columns and big windows, was home to the Brunswig store and pharmacy until 1960. San Diego artist David Robinson added a mural on the south wall.

GASLAMP QUARTER HISTORIC STRUCTURE

14 / **East West Building** (1990)
517 Fourth Ave.
RNP

Contemporizing the traditional brick warehouse, the architects created a sculptural mix of simple geometric forms energized by a curving upper facade that "floats" above the rectilinear ground level—the curve softens the appearance from the street, and the visual impact of this new structure on the historic William Heath Davis House next door. The building is skinned in brick veneer—the thinness revealed to signal that the material is a wrapper, not a structural element. A Japanese courtyard garden in back adds natural light.

15 / **William Heath Davis House** (1850)
410 Island Ave.

Shipped around Cape Horn, this was one of a handful of prefab kit "saltbox" houses that were New Town's earliest structures when the center of the city shifted away from Old Town—developer Alonzo Horton occupied the home in 1867. Originally at State and Market Streets, it was restored and moved by the City of San Diego to its current location in 1984 to house Gaslamp Quarter information offices and museum.

GASLAMP QUARTER HISTORIC STRUCTURE

16 / **Wimmer-Yamada Building** (1982)
516 Fifth Ave.
BRUCE DAMMANN

A simple facade framed in teak respects the district's scale and adds a fresh modern face to a historic block.

17 / **The Baltic Inn** (1987)
521 Sixth Ave.
ROB WELLINGTON QUIGLEY

For some 50 years, downtown San Diego saw no new affordable rental-room hotels, known as SROs. Quigley's 204-room Baltic, with its smart forms and affordable graphic pizazz, proved that "inexpensive" doesn't have to mean "boring".

18 / **Backesto Building** (1873)
614 Fifth Ave.
BURKETT & OSGOOD

The Gaslamp's stateliest retail/commercial building steadies the streetscape with its long, low, horizontal profile and elegant classical detailing. In the early 1980s, the Backesto was among the first buildings restored as the Gaslamp came back to life. GASLAMP QUARTER HISTORIC STRUCTURE

19 / **McGurck Building/Z Gallerie** (1887/1995)
611 Fifth Ave.

When this home furnishings store moved from Horton Plaza to the Gaslamp (into this space designed by Bundy & Thompson), it legitimized mainstream retailing in the historic district. From 1903 to 1984, the space was occupied by Ferris + Ferris drugstore, where Gregory Peck's father worked as night pharmacist.

20 / **I.O.O.F. Building** (1882)
526 Market St.
LEVI GOODRICH

Masons and Odd Fellows shared this two-story Italian Renaissance revival building.

GASLAMP QUARTER
HISTORIC STRUCTURE

GASLAMP QUARTER

21 / **Yuma Building** (1888)
633 Fifth Ave.

ARMITAGE & WILSON

Restored as a live/work loft by interior designer Marsha Sewell (with architects Macy Henderson Cole), the Yuma became a pioneering example of adaptive re-use in the early 1990s; projects like this revived the notion of living downtown. The building was originally owned by a Captain Wilcox, who arrived here in 1849 as skipper of the *U.S. Invincible*.

GASLAMP QUARTER HISTORIC STRUCTURE

22 / **Aztec Theatre/Urban Outfitters** (1905)
665 Fifth Ave.

CLINTON DAY

Originally a meat market (in the old sense), this building became the California Theatre in 1919, and the Aztec in 1930, before becoming a fashion outlet (designed by Pompei) in the 1990s.

23 / **Old City Hall** (1874)
433 G St.

WILLIAM LACY

Italianate details include classical columns and brick arches. Two floors added in 1887 by architects Comstock & Trotsche housed the San Diego Public Library. City government moved here in 1890, with the Police Department on the first floor and council chamber on the fourth. Covered with stucco in the 1950s, Old City Hall was restored during the Gaslamp's renaissance to its original brick and stone (including El Cajon granite).

GASLAMP QUARTER HISTORIC STRUCTURE

24 / **Cole Block Building** (1890)
444 G St.

Albert Cole committed suicide soon after his commercial building was completed. Theopile Verlaque, a pioneering vintner, once ran a liquor store on the corner. GASLAMP QUARTER HISTORIC STRUCTURE

25 / **Gaslamp Pacific Stadium 15** (1997)
701 Fifth Ave.
BENSON & BOHL (EXTERIOR) AND KMA (INTERIOR)

Earlier attempts to in-fill new buildings within this historical district failed, often because of inadequate budgets or poor design. The Cineplex succeeds, with a scale suited to the neighborhood and uplifting Deco-inspired details.

26 / **Llewelyn Building** (1887)
726 Fifth Ave.

Ladies of the night were homeported here during the building's early-20th-century decades, following its early years as the Llewelyn family's shoe store.

27 / **Loring Building** (1873)/**Fritz Building** (1908)
764 and 760 Fifth Ave.

The Renaissance Revival Loring is sibling to the adjacent Fritz. Two facades blend together as one building. The Fritz's lobby features onyx and Tennessee marble. GASLAMP QUARTER HISTORIC STRUCTURE

GASLAMP QUARTER

28 / **Spencer Ogden/DeLaval Building** (1874)
770 Fifth Ave.
WILLIAM LACY

One of the Gaslamp's oldest structures, this French Renaissance tribute features ironwork forged at San Diego Foundry, as well as locally quarried Cajon granite detailing. Realtors, drug stores, a home furnishings outlet, and dentists including "Painless Parker" were among early tenants. GASLAMP QUARTER HISTORIC STRUCTURE

29 / **George Hill Building** (1897)
533 F St.
ZIMMER & REAMER

Built after fire destroyed Horton's Hall, the three-story stone-and-pressed-brick building housed five storerooms and 30 offices. The San Diego State Normal School (now SDSU) had space on the upper floors in 1898; the Isaac Ratner Cap Manufacturing Company, later Ratner's Clothing, once manufactured here. GASLAMP QUARTER HISTORIC STRUCTURE

30 / **St. James Hotel** (1912)
830 Sixth Ave.

When it opened, this was San Diego's tallest building, housing a barber shop, Turkish bath, billiard parlor, and observation room with a prime view of the city. Modern conveniences included hot and cold running water and two high-speed elevators.

31 / **Marston Building** (1881)

801 Fifth Ave.

STEWART BROTHERS

San Diego's first department store was opened in this Italianate Victorian in 1881 by civic father George Marston, who later commissioned planner John Nolen's prescient plans for the San Diego region. The YMCA board (chaired by Marston) and the Prohibition Temperance Union met here in the 1880s. San Diego Federal Savings and the San Diego Building and Loan Association (the first S.D. bank to offer home loans) opened offices here in 1885; after a 1903 fire, the building was remodeled. The city's first gaslamp was installed on this corner in 1885, its first electric arc lamp illuminated here in 1886.

GASLAMP QUARTER HISTORIC STRUCTURE

32 / **Nesmith-Greeley Building** (1888)

825 Fifth Ave.

COMSTOCK & TROTSCHE

This four-story brick-and-granite Romanesque Revival gem features cast-iron pillars that support brick piers. In 1889 and 1890, Mrs. Clara Shortridge Foltz, the first woman admitted to the California State Bar, had her law office here. In the 1910s and 1920s, Asian merchants occupied space here.

GASLAMP QUARTER HISTORIC STRUCTURE

33 / **Louis Bank of Commerce** (1888)

835 Fifth Ave.

CLEMENT & STANNARD

Built by the same siblings as the Hotel Del Coronado, this twin-towered, four-story brick-and-granite Grande Dame is the Gaslamp's most stately Victorian. The ground floor housed a bank, and later an oyster bar frequented by Wyatt Earp. Upstairs was the Golden Poppy Hotel, a brothel run by a fortune teller.

GASLAMP QUARTER HISTORIC STRUCTURE

GASLAMP QUARTER

34 / **Keating Building** (1890)
432 F St.

REID BROTHERS

Cornice bears the name of the original owner's husband George. Steam heat and a wire cage elevator made this a state-of-the-art Victorian office building.

GASLAMP QUARTER HISTORIC STRUCTURE

35 / **Ingersoll Tutton Building** (1894)
832 Fifth Ave.

Corbelled brickwork and Palladian windows contribute to the Romanesque theme here. With its 16-foot ceilings and picture windows, this was the most expensive San Diego building the year it opened: it cost $20,000.

GASLAMP QUARTER HISTORIC STRUCTURE

36 / **San Diego Hardware** (1910)
846 Fifth Ave.

A dance hall and a Woolworth's once operated here; San Diego Hardware is one of the region's few remaining independent home improvement centers, not squeezed out by warehouse chains.

GASLAMP QUARTER
HISTORIC STRUCTURE

37 / **Onyx Building** (1910)
852 Fifth Ave.

Modeled after the Fritz building on Fifth near F, this three-story pressed-brick structure housed offices and apartments upstairs, and retail at the street level, including Cleator's shoestore. Stained glass and green-and-white tiled sign are original. GASLAMP QUARTER HISTORIC STRUCTURE

38 / **Watts-Robinson Building/ Jewelers Exchange**
(1913)
520 E St.
BRISTOW AND LYMAN

This concrete Chicago-style high-rise was one of San Diego's first towers. It housed jewelers amid marble wainscoting, tile floors, and brass fixtures; in the 1980s and 1990s, it was renovated as a restaurant and hotel.

GASLAMP QUARTER HISTORIC STRUCTURE

39 / **Dalton Building** (1894)
939 Fifth Ave.
F.W. STEVENSON

Manhattan Restaurant and Hotel (a hookers' haven) once operated here; the basement was a Prohibition-era speakeasy. In 1930, the building received an Art Deco facelift.

GASLAMP QUARTER HISTORIC STRUCTURE

East Village

Downtown's newest redeveloped neighborhood, East Village is also its most diverse. Originally a Victorian mixed-use neighborhood, later a warehouse district conveniently situated near railroad freight and shipping lines, today East Village is a collection of artists' lofts, new hotels, and new apartments where a new baseball park and central library will be situated. San Diego City College provides an academic anchor for a growing number of technology and communications companies in new offices wired for the future. The New School of Architecture and Woodbury University add two strong design institutions.

Long, low utilitarian warehouse buildings define the rhythms of East Village's streets. Some of the new loft-style residential projects capture the scale and feel of old warehouses, which range from basic boxes to more stylish buildings designed by some of San Diego's most prominent architects: William S. Hebbard, John B. Stannard, Louis Gill, Harrison Albright, Charles and Edward Quayle, Eugene Hoffman, Gustav Hanssen, and William Templeton Johnson.

Although many of its original buildings have been torn down, East Village still has a few fine homes from the Victorian era, when SDG&E built an oil gas manufacturing plant south of Imperial between 8th and 9th Avenues, as well as a forge and blacksmith shop. Original hotels serving visiting businessmen included the Orford, the Lee, and the Clermont. Lawton's Car Hop Restaurant (now a liquor store) on Market Street was San Diego's prototypical drive-in fast food outlet—years before Jack-In-The-Box was born here.

During the 1960s and 1970s, East Village—then known as Centre City East—suffered the same neglect as the rest of downtown, as new development and business interests gravitated to other areas in the region. When redevelopment began in 1975, efforts focused on downtown's core, but later expanded to include East Village.

East Village is well connected to the region at large, with the San Diego Police Headquarters situated here, and the San Diego Trolley cutting through on 12th Avenue. As part of the revitalization effort, this street was designated as an urban boulevard that connects Balboa Park with the waterfront. As such, it was the focus of an urban design effort that added street trees, new landscaping, and public art.

In the past decade East Village has become a vital 24-hour-a-day neighborhood of diverse uses; with its overall density still low, and with much land still eligible for new projects, this area will continue to transform.

East Village Locations

1. **Riviera Apartments**
2. **Timken Building**
3. **Old Main Post Office**
4. **Fletcher-Lovett Building**
5. **Pierrot Theatre/First Baptist Church**
6. **Hotel Mediterranean**
7. **Coliseum Athletic Club/ Jerome's Furniture Warehouse**
8. **Broadway Manor**
9. **The Buckner**
10. **Maryland Hotel**
11. **Arlington Hotel**
12. **Eagles Hall**
13. **Gaslamp Liquor/Lawton's Car Hop Restaurant**
14. **Coast Hotel/Occidental Hotel**
15. **Klauber-Wangenheim Building**
16. **Fire Station #4**
17. **T.R. Produce Warehouse/ Wellman Peck and Company**
18. **Palms Hotel**
19. **Roberto Martinez/ Sheldon Residence**
20. **Mills Building**

E St
F St
G St
Market St
Island Ave
J St
K St
L St

6th Ave
7th Ave
8th Ave

2
10
11
14
15
16

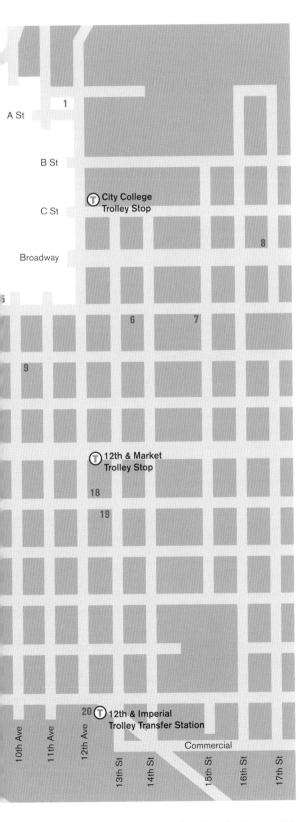

A St

B St

C St

 City College
Trolley Stop

Broadway

1

8

6   7

9

12th & Market
Trolley Stop

18

19

20 12th & Imperial
Trolley Transfer Station

Commercial

10th Ave
11th Ave
12th Ave
13th St
14th St
15th St
16th St
17th St

EAST VILLAGE

1 / **Riviera Apartments** (1928)
1312 12th Ave.

Stepping from five to four stories due to its sloped site, this brick building features horizontal tan brick bands at the roofline and top floor, and raised brick quoins at corners.

2 / **Timken Building** (1908-1910)
861 Sixth Ave.
HARRISON ALBRIGHT

One of San Diego's early Chicago-style buildings, this eight-story reinforced concrete structure was stripped of Albright's original classical exterior details during a 1950s makeover.

3 / **Old Main Post Office** (1936)
815 E St.
WILLIAM TEMPLETON JOHNSON

A grand reinforced concrete public building in the WPA Moderne style of the day, with fluted travertine pilasters and terra cotta reliefs above nine entrances depicting various modes of transport.

4 / **Fletcher-Lovett Building** (1910/1932)
920 E St.

Moved to this location and remodeled in 1932, this three-story brick and steel structure has tall Corinthian pilasters set off by commercial steel windows: ancient meets modern.

5 / **Pierrot Theatre/First Baptist Church** (1912)
906 Tenth Ave.
NORMAN MARSH

This three-story Mission Revival structure has been altered from the original, but this twin-towered building remains (along with downtown's Santa Fe Depot) as a rare San Diego example of that romantic style. It has recently been converted for residential lofts.

6 / **Hotel Mediterranean** (1915)
1327-1331 E St.

Fine and simply detailed box of a neoclassical structure, with clapboard siding and decorative wood bands around the base. Window placement is meticulously ordered; each triple window has a leaded glass transom and a double-hung window on each side of a large fixed window.

7 / **Coliseum Athletic Club/Jerome's Furniture Warehouse** (1926)
1485 E St.
JOHN S. SIEBERT

Before use by San Diego's large discount furniture chain, this was a popular spectator sports venue, with vaulted roofs adding extra space for lighting and seating. Arched doorways and decorative grates are part of the simple Spanish Revival design scheme.

8 / **Broadway Manor** (1912)
1640 Broadway

A three-story Italian Renaissance Revival apartment building is classical in the symmetry of its facade and plan including the centered entrance.

9 / **The Buckner** (1906)
765 Tenth Ave.
S.G. KENNEDY

Combining Craftsman (leaded windows), Italianate (rooftop balustrade), and Victorian (bay windows) elements, this 27-unit apartment building is an example of early-century transitional architecture.

10 / **Maryland Hotel** (1914)
612-650 F St.
W.S. HEBBARD AND FRANK P. ALLEN.

A six-story brick beauty with Italian Renaissance Revival details including corner quoins, and a belt course and cornice lining the top floor, and with steam heat, a central vacuum system, and marble tile floors.

EAST VILLAGE

11 / **Arlington Hotel** (1928)
701 Seventh Ave.

LOUIS GILL

Originally used as a hospital, this three-
story flat-roofed brick building designed
by Irving Gill's nephew stood out as a spare, modernist design, at a time
when neoclassical and Mediterranean influences predominated.

12 / **Eagles Hall**
(1917 & 1934)

733 Eighth Ave.

WILLIAM WHEELER AND
JOHN SELMAR SIEBERT

Three-story stucco-covered brick build-
ing combines Greek-spirited Colonial Revival (instead of the Spanish
mode common to San Diego) and Egyptian Deco elements.

13 / **Gaslamp Liquor/Lawton's Car Hop Restaurant** (1949)
837 Market St.

Before Jack-in-the-Box was
born in San Diego, Lawton's
was one of the first Southern
California drive-ins, an early
sign of the coming culture of the car.

14 / **Coast Hotel/Occidental Hotel** (1887)
501 Seventh Ave.

This wood-frame stucco building
was unusually free of ornamentation for its time.

15 / **Klauber-Wangenheim Building** (1929)
611 Island Ave.

WILLIAM WHEELER

Named for two prominent entrepreneurs and city fathers, the structure is
important as one of San Diego's early International-style warehouses,
sparingly decorated with small reliefs.

16 / Fire Station #4 (1936-1938)

400 Eighth Ave.

GUSTAV A. HANSSEN

Sleek, WPA-funded modern structure of poured reinforced concrete, with a landmark corner tower that serves as a hanging/drying space for hoses. Dentilated freeze and parapet are Deco details.

17 / T.R. Produce Warehouse/ Wellman Peck and Company (1933)

308 J St.

JULIUS KRAFT & SONS

A block-size brick warehouse with Chicago-style steel windows and a rooftop clerestory spine to admit natural light.

18 / Palms Hotel (1889)

509 12th Ave.

Three-story brick-and-wood structure features rectangular, angular, and octagonal bay windows, with Italianate cornices, brackets, friezes, and window mouldings. French Second Empire (think mansard roofs) rooftop towers were removed in the 1920s.

19 / Roberto Martinez/Sheldon Residence (1886)

1245 Island Ave.

COMSTOCK AND TROTSCHE

Quirky Queen Anne by San Diego's leading Victorian-era residential architects, this home is a kaleidoscope of details: fish-scale shingles, angled and square bay windows topped by pediments, and a wraparound porch with turned posts, pediments, and spindlework. The house was moved from 11th and Broadway to this site in 1913; a tower was replaced with a dormer in the 1940s.

20 / Mills Building (1988)

1255 Imperial Ave.

DELAWIE BRETTON WILKES

With its clean lines, this significant transit hub in a revitalizing neighborhood was something of an anomaly when it opened, at a time when frillier postmodernism was still kicking. The Mills Building—which combines offices and retail space with a light rail trolley station and a landmark clock tower—proves once again that form and function can co-exist.

Cortez Hill

Hilltop views drew prominent San Diegans such as Andrew Johnston, John Ginty, Rev. E.S. Chase, Dr. Sarah Winn, and others to build homes here during the 1870s, 1880s, and 1890s—subdividing land once set aside as part of Balboa Park. As plans for the 1915 Panama-California Exposition in the park progressed, apartments and hotels were added: the Sandford, the Arno, the Wilsonia, the Hotel Reiss.

Planner John Nolen's 1926 update of his 1908 regional plan emphasized development of downtown along the waterfront, including a civic mall at the foot of Cedar Street, connecting the seat of government with Balboa Park. With civic attentions turned to Cortez Hill, the El Cortez Hotel and Convention Center, designed by Los Angeles architects Walker & Eisen, was built in 1926—a modern structure with ornate Spanish Colonial details in the spirit of Balboa Park's buildings.

With the addition of the Sky Room and glass elevator in the 1950s, the El Cortez became even more of a land-mark: not only a visible urban icon, but a place where San Diegans dined and shared drinks on special occasions such as marriage proposals, anniver-saries, and graduations, while watching the spectacle of air-planes touching down at Lindbergh Field, and ships pass-ing in and out of San Diego Bay.

By the 1970s, however, other hotels and convention centers were taking business away from the El Cortez, and the once-vital and upscale residen-tial neighborhood had become an affordable rental zone. At various times in the next two decades the hotel was deserted; it was also used by the military and charitable organizations to provide inexpensive lodging. In the early 1980s, the El Cortez was owned and occupied by Morris Cerrullo and his World Evangelism. Several plans for reno-vation and re-use followed, but none materialized until Peter Janopaul and Anthony Block bought the building, renovated it as apartments (removing the 1950s additions to meet historic guidelines), and re-opened it in 1999.

Revival of the Cortez spurred neighborhood revitalization through a combination of historic preservation and major new residential development.

Today, Cortez Hill is a legitimate urban neighborhood again, with homes ranging from rentals to upscale condo-miniums, and architecture spanning 100 years, from turn-of-the-century homes such as the Ginty residence (moved

to its current location in 2001) and the Mills residence sharing the hill with newer developments such as architect/developer Ted Smith's modest mixed residential project to the 22-story Discovery at Cortez Hill condominium tower—which overshadows the El Cortez as the highest building on the hill. Pedestrian-friendly planning elements include the new Tweet Street neighborhood park featuring colorful birdhouses designed by San Diego artists and children.

Cortez Hill is a legitimate urban neighborhood again, with homes ranging from rentals to upscale condominiums, and architecture spanning 100 years.

Cortez Hill Locations

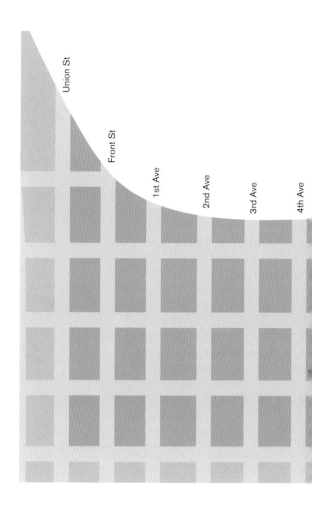

1 **Cortez Hill Transitional Housing**

2 **Ninth and Beech**

3 **CityMark on Cortez Hill**

4 **Soleil Court**

5 **Cortez Hill Park/Tweet Street**

6 **Discovery at Cortez Hill**

7 **Heritage Apartments**

8 **El Cortez Hotel**

9 **Mills Residence**

10 **The Mills at Cortez Hill**

11 **St. Cecilia Chapel**

12 **Dr. W. Peper Residence**

13 **Hearne Surgical Hospital**

14 **Sandford Hotel**

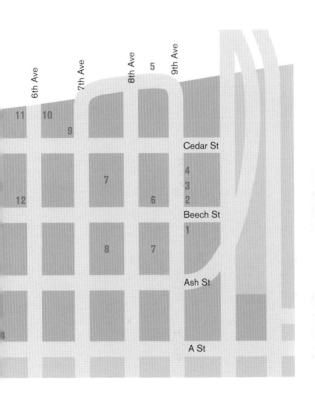

6th Ave
7th Ave
8th Ave
5
9th Ave

11 10
9

Cedar St

4
7 3
2
12 6
Beech St
1

8 7

Ash St

A St

CORTEZ HILL

1 / **Cortez Hill Transitional Housing** (2003)
Ninth Avenue and Beech Street
GOLBA ARCHITECTURE

Here is an imaginative conversion of the old Days Inn Motel, into light-filled modern housing for homeless families.

---

2 / **Ninth and Beech** (1991)
1515 Ninth Avenue
SMITH AND OTHERS

Ranging from small apartments near the corner to spacious townhomes up Ninth, this is another of developer/architect Ted Smith's scrappy in-fills, with an exterior that utilizes common materials in uncommon ways.

---

3 / **CityMark on Cortez Hill** (2002)
1523 Ninth Avenue
MCKINLEY & ASSOCIATES

Sixteen townhomes inspired by East Coast brownstones, the project features pedestrian-friendly stoops and street trees, and, for residents, backyards and roof decks. These "walkups" have underground parking.

Other units are accessible on 10th avenue.

---

4 / **Soleil Court** (2002)
1539-1545 Ninth Ave.
JIM KELLEY-MARKHAM

Mixing Californian and Parisian traditions, these eight townhomes are arranged in a courtyard plan, and feature details such as balconies, recessed windows, and french doors.

5 / **Cortez Hill Park/Tweet Street** (2003)
North of Date Street between Eighth and Ninth Avenues

Artist Candace Lopez conceived the "Tweet Street" public art installation: pole-mounted bird-houses designed by artists and students. On the seam between the dense urb and nearby Balboa Park, this gesture toward Mother Nature is much appreciated.

6 / **Discovery at Cortez Hill** (2002)
850 Beech Street
JOHN PERKINS & CO.

At 22 stories, it's bigger than the historic El Cortez Hotel a block away—but makes a neighborly gesture by stepping back from surrounding streets. Horizontal window bays maximize views, and they are spectacular from this high point in downtown San Diego. A rooftop pool and deck help residents enjoy their panoramic perspective.

7 / **Heritage Apartments** (2002)
750 & 855 Beech Street
TOGAWA & SMITH

Covering two blocks adjacent to the historic El Cortez tower, the Heritage is more noteworthy design-wise for preserving two Victorian houses, than for its 230 new apartments in 4-story structures. Formerly at 1543 Seventh Ave., the Ginty Residence (1886) was relocated to the corner of Cedar and Ninth, renovated, and used by an interior designer as live-work space. The Kroenert Residence (1899), 1471 Eighth Ave., is a prime pre-modernist design by Irving Gill with William Hebbard.

8 / **El Cortez Hotel** (1927)
702 Ash Street
WALKER & EISEN

San Diegans spent many romantic evenings in the Sky Room lounge, added in the 1950s to this 14-story tower. The modern reinforced con-crete building has a Spanish Churrigueresque entry featuring pilasters, ornate capitals, and decorative urns, crests, foliage, and ribbons. In the late 1990s, the Sky Room was removed when the tower was renovated as apartments, with its original red neon sign restored.

CORTEZ HILL

9 / **Mills Residence** (1901)
1604 Seventh Ave.
HEBBARD AND GILL

Another example of pre-modern
Gill, here combining Craftsman
and Prairie influences. The side-
ways gabled roof has a steeper-
than-Prairie pitch. Craftsman
details include exposed, carved
rafter tails and a Granite chimney.

10 / **The Mills at Cortez Hill** (2003)
Cedar Street between Sixth and Seventh Avenues
M.W. STEELE GROUP

New apartments built around the historic Mills residence (1901), a grand
Craftsman mansion on a raised granite foundation, with clapboard siding
and a granite chimney.

11 / **St. Cecilia Chapel** (1928)
1620 Sixth Ave.

An extreme example of
adaptive re-use: this former funeral chapel has
been used in recent years
as a theatrical playhouse.

12 / **Dr. W. Peper Residence** (1894)
1502 Sixth Ave.

Intriguing asymmetrical
design features cross-
gabled roof and diagonal
corner entrance.
Decorative details include
turned porch posts, fish-
scale shingles—it's a quirky
variation of Queen Anne.

13 / **Hearne Surgical Hospital** (1906)

400-420 Ash St.

QUAYLE BROTHERS

Three eyebrow arches crown this eclectic Edwardian-style building, with its base of brick and artificial stone inspired by Chicago's Richardsonian era. Originally a private hospital, the building was renovated in 1973, and has been adapted for office use.

14 / **Sanford Hotel** (1913)

1301 Fifth Ave.

HENRY LORD GAY

Built to house visitors to the 1915 Panama-California Exposition, this u-shaped four-story hotel has decorative cornices and friezes; an arcade that ran along A and Fifth has been partially enclosed. Originally this was an early example of mixed-use development, with three floors of hotel rooms, above ground-level retail/commercial uses.

Little Italy

In 1850, speculators bought 800 acres between Old Town and the New Town being promoted miles to the south by William Heath Davis. Investors including Tennessean Cave Couts, Peruvian Juan Bandini, and Mexican Jose Maria Estudillo, foreshadowing the cross-cultural mix of sights, sounds, cuisines, and architectural details that became Little Italy's calling card. Being speculators, though, the investors held their land for several decades without building.

Lusardi, Piazza, Mosto, Remondino, and Raffin were among the earliest Italian families who came to San Diego during the 1860s and 1870s. By the first decade of a new century the area known as Middletown was populated with Portuguese and Genoese fishing families who founded San Diego's tuna industry. By the late 1930s, the waterfront strip south of Washington Street had a business district, fish canneries, and a residential neighborhood supported by the nearby fishing and aircraft industries. Eventually the concentration of homes and businesses became known as Little Italy.

Italian residents were forced from waterfront homes during the fear of foreigners induced by World War II. The area's original distinguishing architecture consists mainly of residences in late Victorian and early 20th century Craftsman styles. Some of the newer buildings reference the district's heritage, others make no attempt to encompass history.

More than 6,000 families once lived in Little Italy. Construction of Interstate 5 during the 1960s ripped through the neighborhood's heart, destroying an estimated 35% of homes and businesses, prompting 30 years of decline. Through economic ups and downs, including the collapse of the tuna industry, and urbanization, though, the authentic core of Little Italy survived along India between Cedar and Grape, centered around Assenti Pasta, Filippi's Pizza Grotto (formerly a stable and blacksmith shop), Solunto's Bakery, Mimmo's café, and Café Zucchero; Our Lady of the Rosary remains as a symbol of the community's faith.

Despite Little Italy's will to survive, recognition of the district's significance was slow to come. By 1980, when 30 or so buildings were designated as historic, protecting such essential details as facades and tow-

ers, some of the best buildings had already been torn down. Other buildings that give Little Italy its character remain at risk; the area has become a hot spot for downtown housing ranging from small apartments to high-rise condominiums that threaten not only the architectural character of the neighborhood, but its scenic views of San Diego Bay and the shoreline.

Architects including Rob Wellington Quigley (whose La Pensione Hotel replaced the old Bernardino's Dry Good Store and Tait's Market), Ted Smith, Jonathan Segal, and Public designed new residential projects beginning in the late 1980s that proved new buildings, whether contemporary or historical in character, can fit well with the scale and character of this colorful early San Diego neighborhood. To Little Italy's credit, a strong local merchants association has emphasized locally owned businesses and insisted on advising the planning and design of new developments, in order to avoid the kinds of generic chains that have turned other areas of San Diego into theme parkish zones that feel like nowhere or everywhere.

Through economic ups and downs and urbanization, the authentic core of Little Italy survived

Little Italy Locations

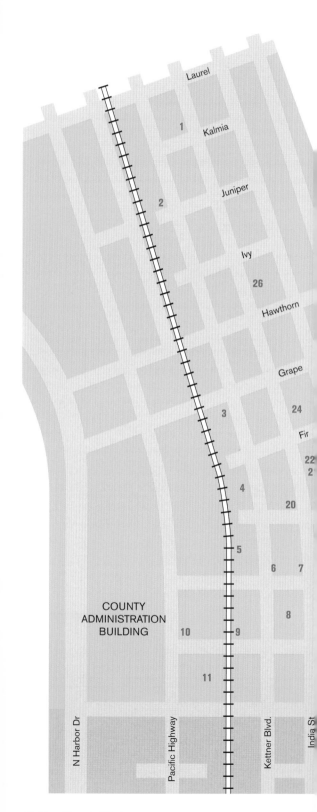

1 McDonough Cleaners/City Dye Works

2 San Diego Macaroni Manufacturing Co.

3 Waterfront Apartments

4 Doma Lofts and Townhomes/
California Stamp Building

5 Camden Tuscany

6 Lusso Lofts

7 Bella Via

8 LIND

9 Standard Sanitary Manufacturing Company

10 Hampton Inn

11 SanDiego Globe Grain & Milling Co./Parron-Hall

12 Village Walk

13 Fire Station/Museum

14 Porto Siena

15 Beaumont Building

16 Our Lady of the Rosary Church and Parish Hall

17 Victorian House Condominiums

18 Amici Park

19 DeFalco's Grocery/San Diego Reader

20 La Pensione

21 Mimmo's Italian Village/Auto Body Company

22 Filippi's Pizza Grotto/Albert Muller Grocery

23 Essex Lofts

24 Milton E. Fintzelberg Commercial Building

25 Vue de L'Eau Apartments

26 India Street Design Center/
San Diego Coffee Co.

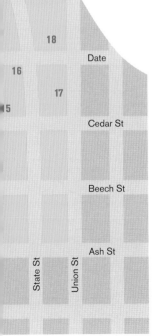

18

Date

16

17

5

Cedar St

Beech St

Ash St

State St

Union St

LITTLE ITALY

1 / **McDonough Cleaners/City Dye Works** (1930)
2400-2404 India St.

An arrow sign signals the corner entry tower (minus its original clock), flanked by tile-roofed wings. Rounded pilasters divide display windows of this commercial Spanish Revival structure.

2 / **San Diego Macaroni Manufacturing Co.** (1924)
2308 Kettner Blvd.

Reminiscent of other waterfront warehouses and aeronautical buildings, this two-story brick warehouse, with its vaulted roof, is the essence of 1920s San Diego.

3 / **Waterfront Apartments** (2001)
Kettner Blvd.
JONATHAN SEGAL

You can't tear down the most popular neighborhood watering hole, so Segal saved the circa-1927 bar, with its glass block Deco entry, and named his 42-loft development after it.

4 / **Doma Lofts and Townhomes** (2003)/**California Stamp Building** (1930)
Kettner Boulevard between Date and Fir Streets
MARTINEZ + CUTRI CORPORATION

Natural light and open plans make these 124 lofts and townhomes flexible and inviting; retail spaces lining Kettner add to the neighborhood's pedestrian appeal. The new project preserved the original California Stamp Company's cool zigzag Moderne tower.

5 / **Camden Tuscany** (2003)
West side of Kettner Boulevard, between Cedar and Date Streets
ARK ARCHITECTS

Mixing 163 apartments with retail space and parking, the building incorporates neighborhood forms and Tuscan colors into a modern scheme that transcends the kitschy norm.

6 / **Lusso Lofts** (2001)
1601 Kettner Blvd.
JONATHAN SEGAL

Next generation urban housing
from downtown rowhome pioneer
architect/developer Jonathan
Segal, this 31-unit project extends
his legacy of pedestrian-friendly modernism.

7 / **Bella Via** (2003)
1608 India St.
CARRIER JOHNSON

Mixed-use residential-retail-com-
mercial creates lively pedestrian
activity. Courtyards help this
building of 41 flats and townhomes maintain some of the
neighborhoods intimate, friendly scale.

8 / **LIND** (1999-2001)
Block bordered by Kettner Boulevard; India, Cedar, and Beech Streets
ROB QUIGLEY ARCHITECTS; SMITH AND
OTHERS; JONATHAN SEGAL; PUBLIC;
ROBIN BRISEBOIS; LLOYD RUSSELL

Redevelopment officials vowed "never
again" when they reached the end of
this harrowing project (LIND stands for

Little Italy
Neighborhood
Development),
which coordinated
six design /devel-
opment teams on
one site to create
healthy variety with 16 row homes
(Segal), 12 affordable rental lofts (Smith
and Public), and 37 low- and moderate-
income apartments (Quigley). Yet, when
the building began picking up awards,
officials were the first to claim credit for
this vital project, which maintains the
scale and urban character of the neighborhood without resorting to
Mediterranean cliches.

LITTLE ITALY

9 / **Standard Sanitary Manufacturing Company** (1911)
726-734 W. Beech St.

Edwardian details such as dentil moldings decorate this three-story building of concrete cast to resemble quarried stone.

10 / **Hampton Inn** (2001)
1531 Pacific Highway
JOSEPH WONG

This homage to the circa-1936 County Administration Center at the foot of Cedar Street is a thoughtful alternative to blockbuster hotels that dominate other downtown locales.

11 / **San Diego Globe Grain & Milling Co./ Parron-Hall** (1909)
820 W. Ash St.

One of the tallest buildings of its day, this concrete, brick, and steel structure is crowned with a gabled ventilating skylight, where dust escaped during production of 20,000 barrels of flour a year.

12 / **Village Walk** (2001)
1501 India St.
MARTINEZ + CUTRI CORPORATION

An explosion of colors and geometric forms that bypasses the scale and historic character of the old Little Italy. This project's prime asset is a public plaza lined with cypress trees.

13 / **Fire Station/Museum** (1915)
1572 Columbia St.

One of Little Italy's few remaining historic public buildings, this utilitarian structure has spare Mission detailing. Today it's a museum for early firefighting memorabilia.

14 / **Porto Siena** (2002)
1601 India St.
WITHEE MALCOLM

Tuscan colors, tile roofs, and wrought iron railings come together in this eclectic attempt at infusing this 88-condominium project with authentic Italian flavor.

15 / **Beaumont Building** (1985)
434 W. Cedar
ROB WELLINGTON QUIGLEY

A pale gray presence that echoes twin towers on a nearby Catholic Church, architect Rob Quigley's live-work building contains a top-level penthouse (what views!), Quigley's fourth-floor offices, and leasable space below. It also has the distinction of winning both an Honor Award from his peers and an Onion from a lay public that didn't look at it long enough to see connections to both fine abstract art and the surrounding city.

16 / **Our Lady of the Rosary Church and Parish Hall** (1923)
1654-1668 State St.
GIANNINNI & FERGUSON

This twin-towered community centerpiece has Mediterranean details including tiled roof, arched openings, and ornamental moldings, murals, frescas, panels, and recesses. Ionic columns support statuary flanking the gabled entry—echoes of Italian hilltowns.

17 / **Victorian House Condominiums** (2003)
1632 Union St.
SFERRA-CARNINI

What do genuine Italian architects do in San Diego's Little Italy? They opt for a touch of 19th century Americana—a thoughtful homage to the circa-1887 Oscar Millard Queen Anne Victorian, with its steep roofs and fish-scale shingles.

LITTLE ITALY

18 / **Amici Park** (2001)
State and Date Streets
LANDSCAPE DESIGN: MARIAN MARUM
PUBLIC ART: NINA KARAVASILES

A sort of "town square" created for families, workers, and students from nearby Washington Elementary School, the park celebrates the neighborhood's heritage with a bocci ball court, and with Karavasiles' sidewalk plaques and café tables, which emphasize the fine Italian cuisine that ties the neighborhood together. Her tables carry recipes in relief on bronze place settings, from which visitors can rub off copies of favorite local recipes using paper and pencil.

19 / **DeFalco's Grocery/San Diego Reader**
1703 India St.

Formerly a neighborhood grocery, now home to San Diego's independent alternative weekly, the building is a humble box-like Italianate affair with clay tile roof trim, and pilasters crowned with bulb-shaped capitals.

20 / **La Pensione** (1991)
600 and 606 W. Date Street
ROB WELLINGTON QUIGLEY

Rather than saving the worn-out Tait's Meat Market building that had been a neighborhood social hub, Quigley recreated the facade along India Street as part of a new four-story building that combines an 80-room single-room-occupancy hotel and two street-level restaurants that have sidewalk tables. Bernardini building also replaced.

21 / **Mimmo's Italian Village/Auto Body Company** (1927)

1743 India St.

Three arched bays pierce the parapet front facade, which hides a flat roof. The building housed an auto body shop, an aircraft parts warehouse, and a washing machine parts company, before becoming an Italian deli famous for its epic "grab-n-go" submarine sandwiches served amid murals of Italian villages.

DOWNTOWN HIGHLIGHT

County Administration Center

(1936)

1600 Pacific Highway

ARCHITECT:
LOUIS GILL, SAM HAMILL, RICHARD REQUA, WILLIAM TEMPLETON JOHNSON

San Diego's finest civic architecture (not counting Balboa Park) is a WPA-era classic designed by a team of four top architects. Conceived as a Spanish Revival design in the spirit of Balboa Park, the center evolved into a simpler, beautifully proportioned building in the popular 1930s "moderne" style also used for Los Angeles Public Library and Nebraska's state capital building in Lincoln (both by Bertram Goodhue, chief architect for Balboa Park). The landmark tower was scaled back from 225 to 150 feet, due to air traffic and budget concerns. Get out of your car to view exquisite details: Spanish tiles designed by Chicago architect Jess Stanton, fluted plaster mouldings that emphasize the tower's verticality, and, on the west side, sculptor Donal Hord's "Guardian of Water" fountain. John Nolen's urban master plan (1908, 1926) envisioned this building as the seat of a government mall along Cedar Street, but other public buildings never materialized here.

LITTLE ITALY

22 / Filippi's Pizza Grotto/ Albert Muller Grocery (1914/1939)
1747-1753 India St.

Nothing fancy here, but plain white stucco walls, a colorful awning, simple signage, a tiled parapet evoke the humble architecture of Italian villages.

23 / Essex Lofts (2002)
NW corner of State and Fir Streets
SMITH AND OTHERS

With this 36-unit project, architect/developer Ted Smith continues the style-on-a-budget aesthetic he pioneered with the Merrimack Building on nearby Beech Street, and in Del Mar in North County. His neighborly "blendo" approach borrows forms and materials from adjacent buildings.

24 / Milton E. Fintzelberg Commercial Building (1928)

1917-1921 India St.
Concrete-and-brick structure once housed the Avalon movie theater, but the original marquee is long gone. Unadorned pilasters symmetrically divide the front wall, along with four evenly spaced arched windows.

25 / Vue de L'Eau Apartments (1913)
550 W. Grape St.
Craftsman and Mission Revival elements merge in this four-story stucco apartment complex.

26 / India Street Design Center/
San Diego Coffee Co. (1926)

2141-2165 India St.

Two-story brick building combines a warehouse scale and appearance typical of this neighborhood, with more intimate details such as storefront bays defined by brick pilasters and shaded by canvas awnings, and smaller second-floor windows.

Balboa Park

San Diego's greatest triumph of urban planning came in 1868, when the city set aside 1,400 acres as permanent open space just north of downtown. At the time, the context was suburban – more "country" than "city". Today, however, Balboa Park is the cultural and recreational centerpiece of the sixth largest American city–an urban open space and greenbelt as significant to San Diego as Central Park is to New York.

The need for open space was recognized at the outset of downtown development. In 1868, a year after Alonzo Horton acquired 168 downtown acres where he hoped to build a new town, city fathers set aside 1,400 raw, native acres as park land.

"Canyons and mesas were covered by dense chaparral and after winter rains the arid land bloomed in large patch-

es of yellow, white and blue with the many small flowers of wild adenostema, sage brush, 'Spanish' violets, shooting stars, mimulas and white popcorn," wrote Gregory Montes in the *Journal of San Diego History.* "The low-lying vegetation was home to coyotes, wildcats, rabbits, squirrels, quail and lizards."

In 1890, more than 10,000 trees (blue and sugar gums, acacias, pepper trees, fan palms, cypresses) were planted on the 100-acre Howard Tract between Cabrillo and Florida Canyons, and the Ladies Annex of the San Diego Chamber of Commerce planted 700 additional trees and shrubs including eucalyptus, Monterey cypress, acacias, pines, flame trees, and poinsettias along the park's western edge. In 1892, Kate Sessions was granted a free 10-year lease for 32 acres and free water in exchange for creating a public nursery, and planting and maintaining 100 trees in the park each year.

Sessions knew Frederick Law Olmsted's pastoral landscapes in Central Park and elsewhere, and hoped to combine her horticultural ideas with a park plan by a leading landscape architect. She knew that with it's temperate climate, San Diego would support palms, bamboos, cacti, bougainvillea, eucalyptus, pepper trees, poinsettias, and other plants from around the world.

In 1902, the city retained Samuel Parsons, Jr., a protégé of Olmsted and believer in naturalistic planning and landscape design, in letting terrain dictate development. Parsons "warned that when landscape architects created streams and lakes where there was no natural flow of water or when they filled in valleys and canyons formed by nature the results would be disastrous," according to histo-

rian Richard Amero. "Parsons proposed that peripheral roads and bands of trees should define the park's borders. In contrast to straight peripheral roads that would carry through traffic, paths and roads within the park would wind around natural contours, would open surprise views, and would pass along highlands at the edges of canyons. Recognizing that rainfall was scant in Southern California, Parsons advised planting water-consuming grasses in small plots at park entrances. He suggested naming these entrances after trees grouped there, such as Pepper Tree, Blackwood Acacia, Monterey Pine, and Torrey Pine.

"To accentuate wild flowers and to dramatize vistas, he proposed keeping trees on mesas low. Nevertheless, to provide enclosure and to frame views, he would allow eucalyptuses at strategic points on the mesas. Because cuts and fills would mar the contrast between mesas and canyons, he cautioned against them. To intensify the sense of depth in the canyons, he would plant trees in the canyons rather than on the mesas. These trees would become taller as they approached the canyons' rims…he advocated preserving native plants where 'they made the best display,' and…emphasized that flower beds and buildings should be few and that they should be located in the southern portion of the park." According to historian Montes, Balboa Park's "design and uses," at this point, "were linked more closely than ever to an unbroken chain of 19th- and 18th-century Anglo-American public parks and landscaping tradition from Frederick Law Olmsted to Andrew Jackson Downing, Sir Joseph Paxton, John Nash, Humphrey Repton, William Kent, and Lancelot Brown."

San Diego's population was 39,000 in 1909, when Chamber of

Commerce President G. Aubrey Davidson proposed an internationl expo to celebrate the 1915 christening of the Panama Canal. When San Francisco announced its own expo, San Diego decided on a fair with a regional flavor. "City Park" was renamed "Balboa Park" in 1910, in honor of the explorer who crossed Panama in 1513 and reached the Pacific Ocean.

Despite the significant amount of planning already accomplished by Parsons, the expo committee first choice as master planner for the new expo grounds was Daniel Burnham, founder of the City Beautiful movement and planner for the 1893 World's Columbian Exposition in Chicago. But Burnham was too busy, so San Diego instead retained the Olmsted Brothers—Massachusetts planners and landscape designers, sons of John Olmsted, the patriarch of modern landscape planning who was responsible (with Calvert Vaux) for Central Park in New York. Frank P. Allen, known for his orderly management of an earlier Seattle fair, became director of works for San Diego's expo.

In choosing a lead architect for the expo, the Olmsteds vetoed local favorite Irving Gill, whose spare Mission modernist style was, along with Berkeley architect Bernard Maybeck's designs, one of the earliest examples of regional modernism in California. Instead, the position of fair architect was awarded to New Yorker Bertram Goodhue, who had lobbied hard for the commission.

"I suppose…they have got some incapable local talent for the job, which was, I suppose, no more than could be expected, since human nature in California is very much like human nature everywhere, only perhaps more so," Goodhue wrote, prior to his selection. "I am sorry too for the San Diegans because I consider myself quite a shark on the sort of stuff (Spanish Colonial style) they ought to have and am pretty familiar with California conditions." After prominent architects helped Goodhue with letters of support, San Diego hired him in 1911.

Goodhue discards Olmsted plan

The Olmsted plan concentrated buildings and activities north of San Diego High School.

"A 250 foot wide formal avenue, the 'Plaza Larga' (Long Plaza), extending for almost a quarter mile, was to have been flanked by twenty-five foot wide, arcaded sidewalks and behind them, as this was still pre-Goodhue, several 'Spanish Mission' style exhibition buildings," according to a historical account. "The Plaza Larga ended in a three-acre square, the 'Plaza de Musical' also arcaded and surrounded by several major buildings in the Mexican colonial and Spanish style of a 'Plaza Mayor' (Main Plaza). North and

San Diego Historical So
sandiegohistory.

east of the formal Plaza de Musical the Olmsted plan adapted to a small canyon with informal, curving, 'Picturesque' paths leading to foreign government buildings and a terraced, formal Hispano-Moorish garden with cascades and fountains, modelled somewhat on the Alhambra's Generalife Garden at Granada. The extensive waterworks were to be fed by a fifty million gallon reservoir at the top of the hill near the present Naval Hospital parking lot."

Olmsted and Goodhue made several revisions to this plan. They changed building locations and landscape details to cut costs, enhance views, accommodate a changing list of exhibitors, and incorporate the switch in architectural style from Gill's spare approach to Goodhue's Spanish Colonial.

But Goodhue's ultimate vision was for a more elaborate, higher-profile expo. He decided to concentrate on the site's central mesa, instead of the canyon to the south. Ultimately, the Olmsted notion of a pastoral escape from the city lost out to Goodhue's more formal collection of buildings, exhibits, and gardens. Goodhue and Frank P. Allen then developed the park layout that survives today, organized around the east-west promenade known as the Prado.

Goodhue's Spanish "dream city"

Watercolor renderings of the 1915 expo depict

Goodhue's dreamy vision for the park, and show how San Diego began to be romanticized for marketing purposes, along the same lines as Los Angeles was sold with pastoral images of orange groves on packing crate labels and real estate brochures.

Goodhue felt that the blockbuster scale of international expos in

America overshadowed any sense of place or local character—he believed San Diego to be among the world's most inviting regions:

"The Riviera, the bays of Naples and Salerno, some of the Greek Islands, certain mountain valleys in India, the Vega of Granada, the parallel one of Shiraz….(but) in Southern California may be found every attraction possessed by those cited—the tenderest of skies, the bluest of seas, mountains of perfect outline, the richest of sub-tropical foliage, the soft speech and unfailing courtesy of the half-Spanish, half-Indian peasantry." During the 1915 expo, Goodhue recalled in a memoir, "everything that met the eye and ear of the visitor were meant to recall to mind the glamour and mystery and poetry of the old Spanish days…

"Between the site and that boundary of Balboa Park from which it is most effectively and readily reached, runs a great cleft in the earth, the Canon Cabrillo. Any approach from the west must cross this canon, so, quite as a matter of course, we all visualized a bridge whose eastern end should terminate in a great pile of buildings that should be at once the crux of the whole composition and, with the bridge, should ever remain the focal and dominant point of the city when the Fair, and even the memory of the Fair, had passed utterly."

As a fantasy, the expo was intended as a temporary installation, "for it must be remembered," Goodhue wrote, "that Exposition Architecture differs from that of our everyday world in being essentially of the fabric of a dream—not to endure but to produce a merely temporary effect." Yet several generations of San Diegans successfully fought to preserve the original buildings and gardens—perhaps their efforts have been symptomatic of a region more comfortable with a romanticized past than a modern present and future.

Today, when one walks or drives into Balboa Park over the bridge described by Goodhue, the experience is dramatic transition from the urban realm to a pastel-hued dreamscape.

Beyond the bridge are the California Building's brightly tiled dome and ornately decorated tower—the tower was the first of many towers that would become the region's defining icons and landmarks. The bridge marks the entry to a pedestrian promenade—the Prado—that anchors a Beaux Arts-style axial site plan. Hundreds of yards down this mall to the east, the axis culminates in a fountain with a spire of water that serves as the California Tower's counterpoint.

In most accounts of Southern California's architectural history, it is usually the Los Angeles modernists who are credited for exploiting the intimate connections between indoor and outdoor spaces, between rooms and gardens or courtyards or patios, made possible by temperate weather. But while Goodhue's architectural leanings were traditional, his ideas about responding to climate laid the foundation for generations of regional modernism.

"Only in such a climate and amid such surroundings are open-air concerts possible, therefore, the Great Organ, that was the gift of one of San Diego's most munificent citizens, would remain, faced by its auditorium surrounded by trees and open to the stars. And so, too, would the Botanical Building, under whose protecting treillage grow in rank luxuriance the plants of other and hotter countries.

"In the introduction to a book dealing with the buildings of an exposition," Goodhue concluded, in the years before the second Balboa Park expo, "it is perhaps strange to say quite flatly that so many buildings that have given pleasure to so many should be destroyed; but, after all, this was the paramount idea in the minds of the fair's designers, and only by thus razing all of the temporary buildings will San Diego enter upon the heritage that is rightfully hers."

1935: Richard Requa amends the dream

Twenty years after the first expo established Balboa Park, San Diego presented a more extravagent reprise, with San Diego architect Richard Requa assuming the supervisorial role occupied by Bertram Goodhue for the first expo.

"The Exposition of 1935 represents the full flowering of the ideals which motivated our earlier effort, said G. Aubrey Davidson, president of the first expo, chairman of the board for the second. "In the building of this exposition Mr. Richard Requa figured as the presiding architectural genius. The manner in which he interpreted Mr. Goodhue's architecture scheme in terms of a series of buildings representing a complete history of the Southwest, presents an eloquent testimonial to his great ability and artistry."

According to Requa, "I turned, for ideas and inspiration, to the perhistoric and native architecture of the Southwest, studying the Indian Pueblos and the architecture developed to such a wonderful state of perfection in Mexico and Yucatan by those mysterious early inhabitants, the Aztecs and the Mayas."

Relying on his travels through Morocco, Algeria, and other Mediterranean places, Requa added authentic architectural and landscape details, including the House of Hospitality's new courtyard and Casa del Rey Moro Garden (both of which required significant alterations to Winslow's original design, including removal of a south wing(both of which required significant alterations to Winslow's original design, including removal of a south wing). Also new in 1935 was the Alcazar Garden.

Requa's plan for the 1935 expo expanded the park's building program onto a mesa southwest of the Organ Pavilion. The new area was named "the Palisades" and included the Palisades Building, the New Mexico Building, the House of Pacific Relations, the Ford Building, the Municipal Gymnasium, and the Federal Building.

Requa's own designs of regional-flavored buildings included Spanish Village, intended to replicate real everyday buildings and spaces, and the Pueblo-style Palisades Building. Requa also designed the Moderne Conference Building and Municipal Gymnasium.

Whatever has been said of Requa's eclectic approach, he brought thorough historical knowledge and a commitment to authenticity to his job as director of expo architecture.

To see the evidence, visit the San Diego Historical Society in the park and ask for Requa's oversize limited edition leather-bound travel journals, which include his own photos, sketches, and diary entries from his visits to foreign lands.

Also to his credit, Requa recognized—perhaps to a greater extent than his predecessor Goodhue—that out-door spaces are as important, maybe more important, than the park's buildings. At the outset, Requa acknowl-edged the thoughtful plant selections and public spaces made in 1915.

"Indeed, the landscaping had become the outstanding fea-ture of the whole harmonious ensemble," he wrote in his account of the 1935 expo. "This made apparent the fact that the planting of the trees, shrubs, and vines for the first exposition had been carefully planned for the future and not just for the duration of the fair. This consideration of ultimate results influenced me in the planning of garden features for the new exposition. Not only must they har-monzie with the present planting but they should also be permanent additions to the park enhancing the charm of the whole, through the years to come."

"In my travels about the world, I had found three gardens of outstanding interest and beauty. They are all what I call architectural gardens. Gardens that were designed and built, not just graded and planted; gardens that were inti-mately associated with and really an integral part of the buildings that adjoined them; gardens that were really planned to be furnished and lived in, as an outdoor addi-tion to the building—not merely an improvement of the plot surrounding the structure."

In the future

In the decades since the 1935 expo, several controversies have come to Balboa Park. As recently as the 1970s, it seemed significant original buildings could be lost to neg-lect. But the 1990s reconstruction of the House of Hospitality and House of Charm sealed the city's commit-ment to preservation in the park. Meanwhile, landscapes that dated from both expos had been altered with careless or inappropriate plantings, and original plantings had been neglected to an extent that they obscured the buildings. As part of architect Milford Wayne Donaldson's House of Hospitality restoration, landscape architects Garbini & Garbini restored the building's gardens. The Botanical Building has also been restored with all new redwood lath. Over the years, Highway 163 through the park has been preserved as a greenbelt.

San Diego has employed some of the region's most capa-ble planners to map out the park's future—there is still much vacant land that could be developed, especially the expansive East Mesa across Park Boulevard from the park proper. The intrusion of autos has sparked much debate.

Auto traffic has been excluded from some areas, while debate continues as to how or where new parking might be added. Planners have also addressed various proposals to expand the adjacent San Diego Zoo.

Smitten with Goodhue's Spanish Colonial dream, San Diego has occasionally gone overboard in its attempts to hue to and even expand the original themes. In the 1990s, a particularly questionable addition was made to the park: a freestanding arcade in front of the modernist Timken Museum that preservationists claimed was true to 1915 (the Timken's predecessor included an arcade). Rather than enhancing the park's historical aura, the arcade seems more like an attempt by old-school purists to make the Timken invisible with a faux flourish that skeptics refer to as "facade-omy". At the same time, the park (perhaps reflecting the attitudes of the city at large) has not evolved with the times. Architect Rob Quigley's new Activity Center (across Park Boulevard from the rest of the park) is the only truly contemporary design.

If Balboa Park is considered the region's prime cultural respository, then it ought to include some evidence that creativity is alive and well. But it is difficult to imagine Balboa Park ever gaining the equivalent of I.M. Pei's pyramid at the Louvre in Paris—San Diego has never been very comfortable with the notion that the past and present can peacefully co-exist. Balboa Park, and to a large extent the art presented there, reveals a region that has always been most at home with the status quo.

Balboa Park Locations

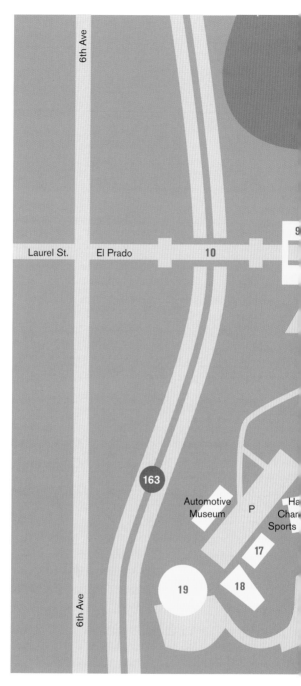

1 **Spanish Village**

2 **Natural History Museum**

3 **Casa Del Prado**

4 **Casa de Balboa**

5 **Botanical Building + Lily Pond**

6 **Timken Museum**

7 **San Diego Museum of Art**

8 **Old Globe Theatre**

9 **California Building/Museum of Man**

10 **Cabrillo Bridge**

11 **Alcazar Garden**

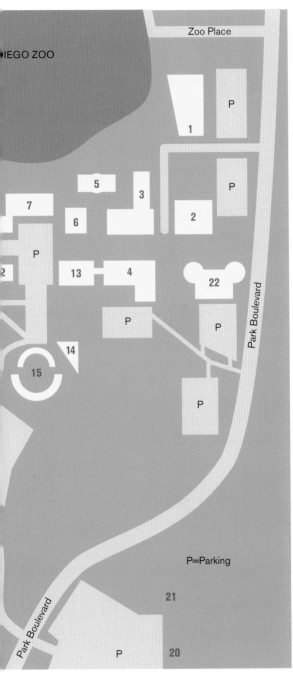

12 House of Charm/Mingei Museum

13 House of Hospitality

14 Japanese Friendship Garden

15 Spreckels Organ Pavilion

16 House of Pacific Relations

17 Municipal Gym

18 Ford/Starlight Bowl

19 Ford Building/Aerospace Museum

20 Naval Hospital

21 Balboa Park Activity Center

22 Reuben H. Fleet Science Center

1 / **Spanish Village** (1935)

RICHARD REQUA

Monumental public buildings inspired by the Spanish Colonial era are well represented along the park's Prado—but Requa also wanted the second expo to offer glimpses of the simpler architecture of everyday life. "Such were the shops, and dwellings of the humbler citizens, not ostentatious but none the less interesting in the naïve expression of native art," Requa wrote in his personal account of planning the expo. "We therefore provided examples of this more intimate phase of the picture of the times in the Spanish Village and in the group of cottages forming the House of Pacific Relations." Situated at the northern edge of the park, near San Diego Zoo, Spanish Village has been the subject of much debate as to whether it should be redeveloped—but changing the look and character of the Village would deprive the park of a folk-art enclave representative of California and Baja's simpler times.

2 / **Natural History Museum** (1933 + 2000)

WILLIAM TEMPLETON JOHNSON/BUNDY & THOMPSON

Only one wing of Johnson's original two-sided design was built, causing a space crunch that persisted until a millenial expansion doubled the museum's size. Johnson's museum is an oddity among park buildings designed by Goodhue—consistently praised for their historical detail and pedestrian-friendly planning. Johnson's museum, by contrast, has a second-story entry that forces visitors to scale a grand staircase. Between its awkward access and monumental scale, the Natural History Museum makes no connections to Goodhue's carefully crafted system of arcades, gardens, and public spaces (nearby is the Plaza de Balboa Fountain designed by Delawie, Macy & Henderson with Wimmer Yamada in 1972). According to historian Richard Amero, "the main facade of the Natural History Museum is a hodgepodge of inharmoniously related trivia [ranging from bison heads to Egyptian cats and sea horses] that does nothing to dramatize the contents inside the building." At the new millenium, Bundy + Thompson designed a major addition.

San Diego Zoo

(1916)

2900 Zoo Dr.

Launched as a rambling series of cages along Park Boulevard that provided a sideshow to the 1915 expo in Balboa Park, the zoo eventually grew into one of the world's largest, with buildings designed by a variety of leading architects. Louis Gill (Irving's nephew) designed the first aviary. Lloyd Ruocco added a building in the Children's Zoo. Tucker Sadler Bennett designed the Otto Center, and several exhibits were designed by Delawie Macy Henderson. Contemporary exhibits (designed under the direction of Zoo Architect David Rice) include Larson Carpenter's Panda Research Station and Dale Jenkins' Heart of the Zoo.

3 / **Casa Del Prado** (1971)

WHEELER WIMER

Known originally as the Varied Industries and Food Products Building (designed by Carleton Winslow in 1915), this L-shaped Spanish Colonial structure featuring a church-like entrance marked by twin towers crowned by blue-and-yellow tiled domes was the largest of the "temporary" expo buildings. Slated for destruction following the fair, the building was spared during World War I, when it became a military barracks and post office. For the 1935 expo, this became the Food and Beverage building. With reliefs commemorating Father Junipero Serra, the north wing was known as "the church". The south wing includes decoration made from the same molds as on the north, with the addition of seeds, fruits, vegetables, and other agrarian/fertility myth imagery. The east facade served as a surrogate San Simeon in Orson Welles's "Citizen Kane". Campaniles that originally distinguished each wing were not replicated in a 1970-1971 reconstruction that added a second floor and patio within the south building, as well as an open-air patio between the wings.

4 / **Casa de Balboa** (1915)

WHEELER WIMER

Architect Carleton Winslow's Spanish Renaissance proposal lost out to an eclectic scheme from architect Frank Allen that combined Venetian elements with corner pavilions (dramatically crowned by finials) modeled after a 17th century mansion in Queretaro, Mexico. Despite its haphazard borrowing, the building makes high romance: along the Prado, first-floor arches make this building a part of the arcade through the park's center, beneath second-story balconies with wrought-iron railings and richly detailed mouldings. The tiled roof floats fantastically above it all, supported by kneeling nudes. Although modern architecture wasn't big in 1930s San Diego, L.A. modernist Richard Neutra designed a prefab 20-by-60-foot steel structure erected for the 1935 expo behind the then-Palace of Better Housing. Following destruction by a fire in 1978, the building was reconstructed and renamed "Casa de Balboa." It now houses The San Diego Historical Society, the Model Railroad Museum, and the Museum of Photographic Arts.

5 / **Botanical Building + Lily Pond** (1915)
CARLETON WINSLOW

When it opened, this steel-framed, bent-redwood enclosure was the largest wood lath building in the world—250 feet long, 75 feet wide, 60 feet tall. The steel frame was originally intended for a railroad station; expo planners got it at a bargain price. Renovated at the turn of the new millenium, the building contains more than 2,100 permanent plants as well as changing displays; the adjacent 250,000-gallon lily pond is decorated with dozens of floating water lilies and lotus plants.

6 / **Timken Museum** (1965)
FRANK L. HOPE

When the art collections of the Timken and Putnam families were home-less in the 1950s, the only modern building along the Prado was built—against protests from purists who favored consistency with the architec-ture of the expos in 1915 and 1935. City leaders initially seemed to favor a historical design, but approved the modern proposal, afraid that the col-lections would end up elsewhere. Although controversial, the building is a solid example of spare modernism and contains excellent, well-lit galleries. To make way for it, the once-grand Home Economy Building by architects Carleton Winslow and Bertram Goodhue was demolished—a loss that tra-

ditionalists tried to partially recoup in the 1990s by reconstructing an arcade along the Prado (in front of the Timken) where the Home Economy Building's arcade once con-nected it to the rest of the park.

7 / **San Diego Museum of Art** (1926)
WILLIAM TEMPLETON JOHNSON

One of San Diego's most prolific architects (from San Diego Trust & Savings downtown to Serra Museum in Presidio Park and several houses), Johnson had never before designed a museum when he was awarded this job. Enclosing the north end of the park's Plaza de Panama, this is one of the most prominent sites within the park's axial Beaux Arts plan. Johnson trained at the Ecole des Beaux Arts in Paris from 1908 to 1911, and became one of San Diego's major proponents of Spanish Revival-style architecture during the 1920s and 1930s. His Fine Arts Gallery, as it was called initially, is more restrained in its detailing than other park buildings. It features tile roofs, windows surrounded with cast stone moldings, and a main entry ornamented with busts of Spanish painters Ribera and El Greco, miniature statues of Donatello's "St. George" and Michelangelo's

"David," and reliefs of galleons and shields of Spain, the United States, and California, plus a city seal above the U.S. shield. Statues of painters Murillo, Zurbaran, and Velazquez are mounted in niches above the entry. The west wing (designed by Mosher & Drew) was added in 1966; and an east wing including 25,000 square feet of exhibit space, in 1970.

8 / **Old Globe Theatre** (1982)

LIEBHARDT & WESTON

Modeled on Shakespeare's London Globe, Balboa Park's Globe (1935) was destroyed by an arson fire in 1978, rebuilt, and re-opened in 1982. Originally an open-air venue intended as tempo-rary, the Globe was upgraded to meet building and fire codes, and received a roof, in 1936.

9 / **California Building/Museum of Man** (1915)

BERTRAM GOODHUE

No other structure has defined San Diego's identity as much as this build-ing's romantic tower, often pictured on postcards and in travel articles. Visible from within the park as well as out in the surrounding city, the tower provides a comforting sense of place and serves as an orienting landmark. Up closer, the tower's companion dome, covered with chromatic tiles, resonates with the power of Renaissance-era duomos that anchor many a town square in Latin locales. According to historian Richard Amero, "Goodhue's design amounts to a twentieth century recapitulation of Plateresque, Baroque, Churrigueresque, and Rococo details. It is impure historically and odd in its imposition of a secular window and balustrade on an ecclesiastical frontispiece." Ornamental details include masks, cupids, candelabra, garlands, and fruit—fine, flat ornamentation in the Spanish Plateresque style that originated with silver flatware. Baroque twisted columns and curved mouldings mingle with Rococo scrolls and myriad other details derived from various periods and styles. Prominent fig-ures from San Diego's history are depicted in the decoration, including Father Luis Jayme, a Francisco missionary murdered by Native Americans in 1774; Gaspar de Portola, California's first Spanish governor; and explor-

ers Juan Rodriguez Cabrillo and Sebastian Viscaino, who rediscov-ered the harbor decades after Cabrillo, and named it "San Diego". Although Goodhue beat out native Irving Gill for the job of expo architect, the late historian David Gebhard surmised that the simpler look of Goodhue's subse-quent building's may reflect Gill's influence.

10 / **Cabrillo Bridge** (1914)

FRANK P. ALLEN, JR.
THOMAS B. HUNTER, ENGINEER

While convincing directors of the 1915 expo that buildings should be sited where they are – west of the Florida Canyon site proposed by the Olmsteds – Allen also had to demonstrate that it would be cost effective to build a bridge over Cabrillo Canyon. He succeeded, and the 916-foot-long reinforced concrete bridge designed by Allen in Roman aqueduct style provides a dramatic entrance to the park (as well as a dramatic profile visible to motorists passing beneath it on the 163 freeway).

11 / **Alcazar Garden (next to House of Charm)**

Designed by Richard Requa after the gardens of Alcazar Castle in Seville, Spain, this orderly geometric garden defined by boxwood hedges and decorated with turquoise, yellow, and green tiles is planted with some 7,000 annuals that explode with colors throughout the year. Altered over the years, the garden has been restored to Requa's 1935 scheme.

12 / **House of Charm/Mingei Museum** (2000)

Originally the Indian Arts Building (1915)
BSHA WITH M.W. DONALDSON (RECONSTRUCTION)

Designed by Carleton Winslow, the building replicated the Sanctuary of Guadalupe in Guadalajara. Winslow modeled the tower after the Church of Santa Catarina in Puebla, Mexico. Compared with other park buildings, according to historian Richard Amero, the facade "has a grim aspect reminiscent of fortress churches in sixteenth century Mexico," and is not consistent with the "exuberant Baroque and Churrigueresque detail elsewhere on the grounds". A 1990s ground-up reconstruction replicated the exterior, but reconfigured the interior as modern multi-floor office and museum space including new underground levels – instead of the original high-ceilinged exhibition hall. Original elements including doors, window frames, railings, and cobblestones were re-used, while plaster details were replicated in fiberglass-reinforced plastic. Some feel the renovated landscape should have included original Blackwood acacias (circa 1915) instead of replacement cedars (circa 1935). The fear is that the new cedars will eventually obscure the building.

13 / **House of Hospitality** (1915 and 1935)

CARLETON WINSLOW + RICHARD REQUA
M.W. DONALDSON (RECONSTRUCTION)

Designed, like other park buildings, as temporary scenery more than a permanent building, the House of Hospitality has become a romantic darling of the park that merges Winslow's ornate Plateresque details (including coats of arms) with a courtyard garden and landscape inspired by Requa's travels through Morocco and Algeria. Winslow modeled the main facade after the Hospital of Santa Cruz in Toledo, Spain, according to historian Richard Amero. Plantings in 1915 included rows of Blackwood acacias "groomed to look like candles that were interrupted at strategic points by Italian cypresses. Grass and flowers grew in front of the trees. Behind them a hedge of Coprosma covered the railing between the posts of the arcades and Bignonia and Bougainvillea hung down from the pergolas or clamored up the walls of the arcades. Unlike monochrome palaces in Spain and Mexico, color from the plants gave the building a sprightly air." Between expos, the building was nearly demolished many times. Its survival is partly due to the preservation efforts of city father and downtown department store owner George Marston. In 1935, Requa oversaw remodeling and new "architectural gardens," as he called them. He credited Mexican artist Juan Larrinaga, trained in Hollywood film studios, with color renderings and models that gave form to numerous design details, including "ingenious lighting fixtures". Requa created a new Mediterranean courtyard by opening an enclosed hall. Requa and his staff architect Sam Hamill (who also collaborated on the County Administration Center) used the State Museum in Guadalajara as inspiration. At the patio's center is artist Donal Hord's "Woman of Tehuantepec" fountain, surrounded by tropical plants including banana. H.O. Davis's lighting scheme was inspired by Maxfield Parrish. Color-tinted lights played on landscape details, instead of building  facades, adding mystery. Ground-level spaces include a ballroom and a restaurant space where David and Leslie Cohen opened the Prado on New Year's Eve 1999. After decades of neglect that included voter rejection of a park-renovation bond issue in 1987, the city retained preservation architect Milford Wayne Donaldson in 1993. He reconstructed the House of Hospitality from scratch (to 1935 status) around a steel frame (instead of the original wood), and recast original plaster mouldings in durable fiberglass-reinforced concrete. A new basement houses mechanical functions; the makeover included modern elevators, heating, ventilating, fire sprinklers, and air conditioning. As part of the renovation, non-authentic landscaping was removed, and the plant palette was restored to authentic status, with guidance from Garbini and Garbini landscape architects.

14 / **Japanese Friendship Garden** (1999)

UESUGI TAKEO, NAKAJIMA KEN, HIROO KURANO

Symbolizing connections between San Diego and sister-city Yokohama, Japan, the garden's history in Balboa Park dates back to the Japanese Pavilion built for the 1915 expo. The new garden combines Japanese design and craftsmanship (such as the shoji-screened Exhibit House), with ancient landscape principles evident in features including a traditional sand-and-stone garden, a wisteria arbor overlooking the canyon, and a koi pond.

15 / **Spreckels Organ Pavilion** (1915)

HARRISON ALBRIGHT

Amid the Spanish-Colonial romance that predominates in Balboa Park, the 2,000-seat pavilion is a fantasy flight back to ancient times, with a grand arch at centerstage flanked by curved arcades. Rosettes, stars, satyr heads, floral sprays, and musical motifs are among decorative details. But the real centerpiece here is the pipe organ, built by Austin Organ Co. in Hartford, CT, equipped with 4,445 pipes, and said to be the largest outdoor pipe organ in the world.

16 / **House of Pacific Relations** (1935)

RICHARD REQUA

During the '35 expo, these cottages represented houses from colonial phases of Mexico's history, each one furnished with the flavor of the country represented.

17 / **Municipal Gym** (1935)

RICHARD REQUA

The architect's design was intended to reflect a merger of modern and Mayan sensibilities, reflective of the San Diego region's history. Known as the Palace of Electricity and Varied Industries, the building was converted to a gym with hardwood-floored basketball courts, volleyball courts, table-tennis tables, and re-opened in 1939.

18 / **Ford/Starlight Bowl** (1935)

VERN KNUDSEN

Earfuls of irony here—Knudsen, an acoustical engineer and co-founder of the Acoustical Society of America, designed the 4,000-seat outdoor venue for good live sound, but air traffic at nearby Lindbergh Field today makes live performances a test of audience patience.

19 / **Ford Building/Aerospace Museum** (1935)
WALTER TEAGUE

Balboa Park's sole Streamline Moderne building was donated by Ford to house the '35 expo's transportation exhibits, including the major display by Ford. Similar structures were built at the same time for fairs in New York and San Francisco, but this is the only one remaining. Previously located in the park's Electrical Building, the Aerospace Museum re-opened (after a 1978 fire destroyed much of its collection) in 1980 in the Ford Building.

20 / **Naval Hospital** (1922)
2125 Park Blvd.
BERTRAM GOODHUE

After a prolonged battle that lasted through the 1970s, the city and Navy agreed on a land swap. The Navy received city land in order to build a new hospital to the east, in Balboa Park's Florida Canyon. In exchange, the city acquired the original Naval Hospital. Eventually all buildings were demolished except for three: the twin-towered administration building (now occupied by the city's Parks and Recreation department), the chapel (1944, now home to the Veterans Memorial Center & Museum), and a modernist medical library designed by Delawie & Macy, completed in 1968 (now the Native American Cultural Center).

21 / **Balboa Park Activity Center** (1999)
ROB QUIGLEY/WHEELER WIMER BLACKMAN

The park's first new building in 30 years is also its only example of contemporary architecture. Quigley, who has often experimented with concrete a material also used often by Irving Gill—utilized tilt-up concrete slabs, crowned by a bowed roof that echoes the rooflines of earlier San Diego buildings including aviation hangars dating from World War II.

22 / **Reuben H. Fleet Science Center** (1972/1996)
LOUIS BODMER/DELAWIE WILKES RODRIGUES BARKER

To Bodmer's original Omnimax theater and entry, Delawie Wilkes added a grand rotunda, exhibit halls, and meeting rooms, all in keeping with the styles and scale of historical park buildings.

Old Town

Native Americans had occupied the San Diego region for centuries before the area known today as Old Town became its first European-style city, a Spanish-influenced collection of buildings around a plaza. Early buildings include both adobe structures and wood-frame houses—some of them shipped from the East Coast (similar to the Heath-Davis house at Fourth and Island downtown).

According to the "Ordinances of Discovery, New Population, and the Pacification of the Indies" issued by Spanish King Philip II, the site of a new settlement should be "one that is vacant and that can be occupied without doing harm to the Indians and natives or with their free consent—a plan for the site is to be made, dividing it into squares, streets, and building lots, using cord and ruler, beginning with the main square...

"The main plaza is to be the starting point for the town; if it is situated on the sea coast, it should be placed at the landing place of the port, but inland it should be at the center of the town. The plaza should be square or rectangular, in which case it should have at least one and a half its width for length (in San Diego's case, 130-by-280 feet) in as much as this shape is best for fiestas in which horses are used and for any other fiestas that should be held."

Clearly these new towns placed a high priority on the social life of their citizens. In fact, San Diego's initial town center fared better than its first seat of government; while the Presidio declined, the new town grew steadily, until by 1829 there were more than 600 residents and 30 houses in Old Town, loosely arranged around the plaza. But in 1872 a fire destroyed most of the buildings.

Old Town's basic street plan today also reflects the Spanish mandate for town planning, according to Mexican architect and historian Antonio Padilla-Corona's article in the *Journal of San Diego History*: "From the Plaza shall begin four principal streets: One from the middle of each side, and two streets from each corner of the Plaza." Old Town has only five streets—not eight—from each corner.

In early San Diego, however, two usual Spanish institutions were missing: the church and the monarchy. Churches are generally the central feature of Spanish Colonial towns, typically sited at the edge of a plaza in a way that one's attention is directed there. San Diego, by contrast, was a less civilized place: Duhaut-Cilly described Old Town in 1823 as "thirty to forty houses of poor appearance and some badly cultivated gardens." A few years later in *Two Years Before the Mast,* Richard Henry Dana recalled a "small settlement...directly below the fort, composed of about forty dark-brown-looking huts, or houses, and three or four larger ones, whitewashed, which belong to the gente de razon."

Secrets of those early years continue to be uncovered during periodic archaeological digs on the former site of the presidio, below the Serra Museum designed by architect William Templeton Johnson in 1929. In the blocks surrounding the original Old Town, many period buildings have been restored for use as shops, offices, and restaurants. Visiting the old adobes, one can experience some of the inspiration behind the work of 20th-century San Diego architects including Richard Requa, Irving Gill, and Frank Mead, all of whom helped develop a regional style of design.

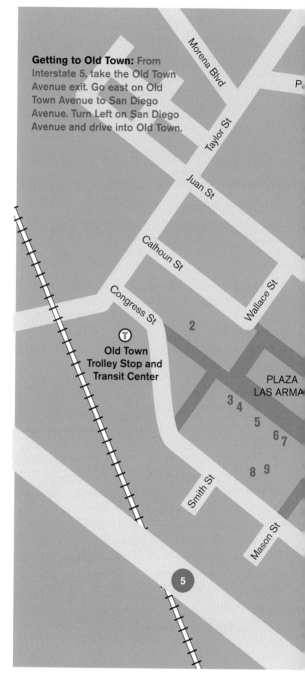

Old Town Locations

Getting to Old Town: From Interstate 5, take the Old Town Avenue exit. Go east on Old Town Avenue to San Diego Avenue. Turn Left on San Diego Avenue and drive into Old Town.

Old Town Trolley Stop and Transit Center

PLAZA LAS ARMA

1 **Serra Museum**

2 **Silvas-McCoy House**

3 **Wrightington House**

4 **Light-Freeman House**

5 **Casa de Machado y Silva**

6 **Colorado House/Wells Fargo History Museum**

7 **First San Diego Courthouse**

8 **Casa de Machado y Stewart**

9 **Mason Street School**

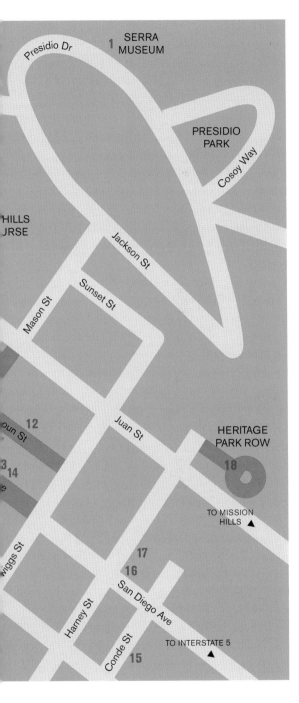

10 **Casa de Estudillo**

11 **Casa de Bandini**

12 **Seely Stables**

13 **Altamirano-Pedrorena House**

14 **San Diego Union Museum**

15 **Old Adobe Chapel**

16 **Whaley House Museum**

17 **Derby-Pendleton House**

18 **Heritage Park Victorian Village**

1 / **Serra Museum** (1929)

2727 Presidio Dr.

WILLIAM TEMPLETON JOHNSON

Designed by San Diego's master of Mediterranean Revival styles, the mission-like museum is situated near where the original mission (moved several miles up Mission Valley) was established. Johnson's design is a masterful composition of view-framing arches, a sanctuary with a high timbered roof, and a tower visible from miles around.

2 / **Silvas-McCoy House** (1869)

Between Congress St. and Calhoun St.

Restored in the 1990s after archaeologists excavated remains of the original two-story wood-frame residence.

3 / **Wrightington House** (early 19th century)

2769 San Diego Ave.

Adobe structure built under Mexican rule, with a wing added in 1852.

When he arrived in San Diego on the ship *Ayucucho* in 1833, Thomas Wrightington became San Diego's first American settler (with the possible exception of Henry D. Fitch).

4 / **Light-Freeman House** (1830)

2767 San Diego Ave.

Adobe saloon and store owned by black pioneers Richard Freeman and Allen Light.

5 / **Casa de Machado y Silva** (1832)
Southwest side of Old Town Plaza facing San Diego Avenue

Spanish Corporal Jose Manuel Machado came to San Diego's presidio in 1782 and built this home in 1832 for his daughter Maria Antonia and her husband Manuel de Silvas. It later served as a boarding house, saloon, restaurant, art studio, souvenir shop, museum and church.

6 / **Colorado House/ Wells Fargo History Museum** (1851)
2733 San Diego Ave.

Formerly a hotel, saloon, and gaming parlor, built by San Diego forefather Cave Couts.

7 / **First San Diego Courthouse** (1847)
San Diego Ave.

Built by the Mormon Battalion that arrived in 1847 to assist the American military effort against Mexico, this was Old Town's first fired-brick structure and served as a townhall, schoolroom, and central government offices.

8 / **Casa de Machado y Stewart** (1830s)
Near northwest corner of Congress and Mason

Mud-brick adobe built by Jose Manuel Machado for his daughter Rosa and her husband Jack Stewart—a shipmate of Richard Henry Dana Jr., whose voyage along California's coast is recounted in his book *Two Years Before the Mast.*

9 / **Mason Street School** (1865)
3966 Mason St.

San Diego's first public school house.

10 / **Casa de Estudillo** (1829)
Between Calhoun and Mason

San Diego's grandest period adobe, featuring 3-foot-thick walls surrounding a courtyard, was restored in 1910 under supervision of Irving Gill's protégé Hazel Waterman. Jose Maria de Estudillo commanded San Diego's presidio, his son Jose Antonio served as tax collector, treasurer, alcalde, and judge under American rule. For many years it was mistakenly identified as "Ramona's Wedding Place" made famous by Helen Hunt Jackson's novel *Ramona*.

---

11 / **Casa de Bandini** (1829)
Corner of Mason and Calhoun

Bandini sailed from his native Peru to California in 1819; he became a Mexican citizen, and later an official in California under Mexican rule. His adobe home was the socio-political hub of Old Town. Later a store, a pickle factory, and motel annex, the Casa is today a popular Mexican restaurant.

---

12 / **Seely Stables** (1869/RESTORED 1970s)
Calhoun St.

Stable and barns housings buggies, wagons, and carriages typical of the time when Albert Seeley ran the San Diego-Los Angeles Stage Line.

---

13 / **Altamirano-Pedrorena House** (1869)
2616 San Diego Ave.

Miguel de Pedrorena came to San Diego in 1842 and married into the Estudillo family. His son Miguel, Jr., built this adobe home (now a bakery) in 1869, and left it to his son-in-law Jose Antonio Altamirano.

---

14 / **San Diego Union Museum** (1851)
San Diego Ave.

Wood-frame structure shipped to San Diego from the East Coast, became the San Diego Union newspaper's first office. Restored to its 1868 condition, including original printroom.

15 / **Old Adobe Chapel** (1850)

3950 Conde St.

This building became San Diego's first parochial church in a new parish in 1858, following secularization of the missions in 1832. It was covered with wood siding in 1889 and restored in 1937.

16 / **Whaley House Museum** (1857)

2482 San Diego Ave.

San Diego's oldest brick structure, now is home to Save Our Heritage Organization.

17 / **Derby-Pendleton House** (1851)

4015 Harney St.

When it was moved next door to the Whaley House, this place is said to have provoked the spirit of Thomas Whaley, which by some accounts still haunts Old Town. George Horatio Derby was a *San Diego Herald* columnist also known as Squibob or John Phoenix.

18 / **Heritage Park Victorian Village**
(1880s and 1890s)

Heritage Park Row

This village is made up of several historic victorians and San Diego's first synagogue. Many of the structures have been moved here from various locations. Buildings include the Senlis Cottage (1896), Sherman-Gilbert house (1887), and Temple Beth Israel (1889).

DOWNTOWN TRANSIT MAP

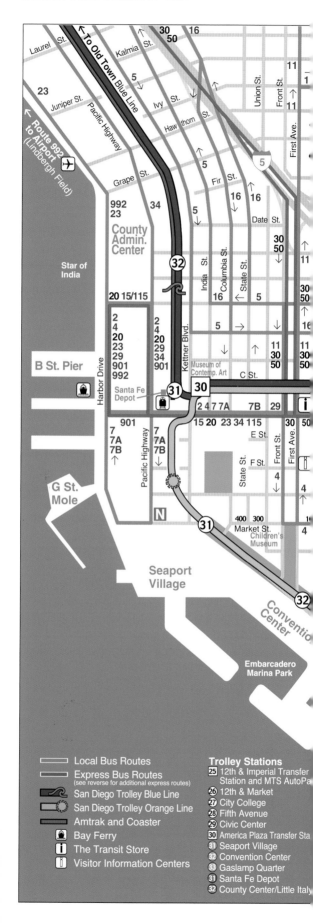

San Diego Zoo

Balboa Dr.

8th Ave. Dr.

Balboa Park

163

7
7B
7A

Sixth Ave.

1
3
25

Park Blvd.

Cedar St.

1
3
25

Beech St.

15
20
115

15
20
115

Ash St.

992

7
7A
7B

Tenth Ave.

Eleventh Ave.

A St.

Symphony Hall

992

23

7
7B

City College

B St.

C St.

992

28

27

Broadway

2

2 7 7A 7B 11 29 901

15 23 30 34 50 115

E St.

Fifth Ave. 800

1
3
5
16
25

F St.

11
29
901

11
29
901

F St.

G St.

G St.

600

500

500 600 700 800 900

3 4 5 16

Sixth Ave.

Seventh Ave.

Eighth Ave.

Ninth Ave.

Tenth Ave.

12th Ave.

26

Market St.

Island Ave.

3 5 16

400

300

1

Eleventh Ave.

13th St.

14th St.

16th St.

J St.

5

K St.

4
11
29

4
11
901

Padres Downtown Ball Park (est. opening 2002)

L St.

Imperial Ave.

1

1

33

25

901

Imperial Ave.

4 11 29

4

To El Cajon and Santee
via Orange Line

r Drive

Commercial St.

National Ave.

11
29

901 902

Logan

0   500   1000 Feet

N
Approximate Scale

© MTDB 2000 8/00

To Tijuana →
via Blue Line

On the Boards

As we wrap up work on this special downtown guidebook, 2004 arrives with an unprecedented volume of new projects in the heart of San Diego—more than at anytime since Centre City Development Corp. was founded in 1975. By the end of this decade, dozens of new developments will add hundreds of new residences, as well as thousands of square feet of new retail and office space. From our architectural perspective, what is noteworthy is some solid urban planning and design: the best of the new projects utilize planning and design ideas encouraged by CCDC, and before that, by urban planning gurus like William Whyte, Jane Jacobs, Lewis Mumford, and in San Diego, John Nolen. Here are a few highlights from among the many new developments in the works downtown:

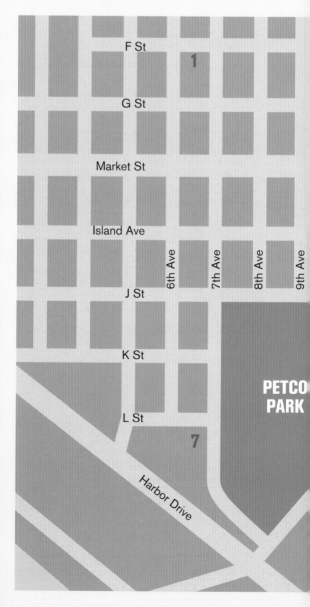

1 / **The Lofts at 777 Sixth Avenue** (2004)

DAVID BAKER ARCHITECTS AND BENSON BOHL ARCHITECTS

At the edge of the Gaslamp Quarter, this well-proportioned mixed-use project proves that new development can co-exist comfortably alongside historic buildings.

2 / **Diamond Terrace** (2005)

Northeast corner Ninth Avenue and J Street

FEHLMAN/LEBARRE AND PERKINS AND COMPANY

Prime project near the new ballpark combines 113 condominiums with 11,000 square feet of retail that should have an invigorating effect on this neighborhood's street scene.

3 / **M2i** (2005)

Block bounded by Market Street and 10th, 11th, and Island Avenues.

MARTINEZ + CUTRI
CORPORATION

Modernist mixed-use
project will bring 230
flexible condominium/
lofts and street-level
retail to the neighbor-
hood near the new ball-
park in East Village.

4 / **Main Library** (2007)

Bounded by Eleventh and Twelfth Avenues and J and K Streets

ROB WELLINGTON QUIGLEY AND TUCKER SADLER NOBLE CASTRO

During public design workshops, participants repeatedly mentioned
domes as design elements they admire around San Diego. Following a
change of site, and several re-designs, the library still has its signature
dome, at the heart of a 10-story building that will counter-balance the
new ballpark with a bold new symbol of knowledge and culture.

5 / **Entrada Apartments** (2004)

Between 13th and 14th on Island Avenue

STUDIO E ARCHITECTS

Finely detailed, modernist residential project, with diagonals,
balconies, and overhangs ener-
gizing the facades.

6 / **Avion** (2005)

Southwest corner of Market and 15th Street

AUSTIN VEUM ROBBINS PARTNERS

With its tapered towers, angular
lines, and expanses of transparent
glass, developer/architect Austin's
project will add visual zest to the
neighborhood, while showing how
architects can command the business side of development.

7 / **Omni San Diego Hotel** (2004)
675 L St.
HORNBERGER & WORSTELL

As East Village evolves into a denser new urban neighborhood, the Omni marks the arrival of the reflective glass high-rise with thoughtful design that makes a sweeping urban gesture with its tower, but greets the street with open, pedestrian-friendly details. A skybridge connects the hotel to the new Padres ballpark.

ON THE BOARDS HIGHLIGHT

Petco Park / Park Blvd. Revitalization

Early last century, urban planner John Nolen envisioned a civic mall downtown—a public promenade connecting a waterfront civic center with the splendors of Balboa Park. Nolen's mall was never realized, but the 21st century will bring a $10.2 million Bay-to-Park link along Park Boulevard. Rather than the multi-block zone imagined by Nolen, this

latter-day link will consist of a more compressed outdoor area on Twelth Avenue, between Broadway and K Street. Here, near the San Diego Padres new ballpark, a landscaped pedestrian promenade with street trees, new lightposts, and public art will serve to connect the ballpark with San Diego's other big park: Balboa Park, San Diego's urban oasis consisting of first-class museums in a lush garden setting. In the heart of redeveloping East Village, where plans include hundreds of new residential units, this new open area will provide the kind of breathing room that makes denser urban development inviting and liveable.

8 / **The Grande At Santa Fe Place** (2005)
1199 Pacific Coast Highway
PERKINS & COMPANY

Twin 39-story towers will be among downtown's tallest and provide spectacular views for buyers of these 444 condos, but are the towers slim enough (and elegant enough) to be nice neighbors along San Diego's waterfront?

9 / **The Pinnacle Museum Tower** (2005)
500 Front Street
AUSTIN VEUM ROBBINS PARTNERS

Strong, straightforward 35-story tower, designed by one of San Diego's leading mid-career architects (Doug Austin). It will be one of San Diego's tallest buildings, and prove that homeboys (and girls) can compete with out-of-town superstars when it comes to high-rise designs.

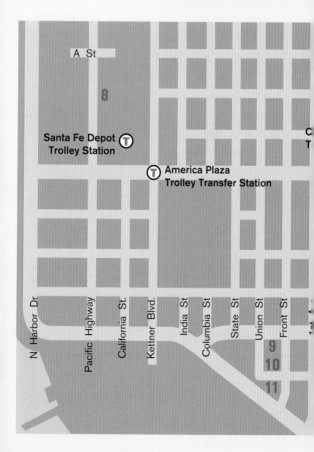

10 / **New San Diego Children's Museum** (2005)
Island Avenue between Front and Union Streets
ROB WELLINGTON QUIGLEY

Quigley's building combines utility, excitement, and great "green" features—particularly the sawtooth roofline that creates long lines of clerestory windows to provide abundant natural light.

11 / **Children's Museum Park** (2005)
Martin Luther King Jr. Promenade west of Front Street
SPURLOCK POIRIER

Inventive design creates an "art for play" space featuring changing environments created by the Children's Museum's artists-in-residence.

12 / **Ninth And Broadway** (2005)
BUNDY & THOMPSON

Straightforward design of a 12-story, 394-unit residential building shows how solid design and exciting color can provide good results on a modest budget.

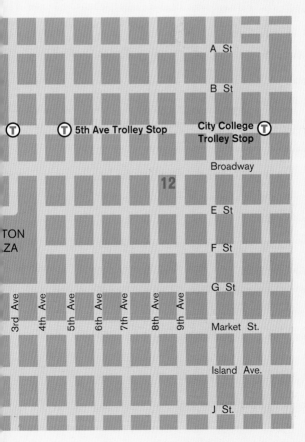

GUIDEBOOK PROJECT TEAM

Photography Team

Neil Larson, AIA
Photography Chair

Zachary Adams

Tom Anglewicz, AIA

Gerardo Arroyo

J. Paulino Caballero

Mike Campos

Kevin Carpenter

Todd Carpenter

Wallace Cunningham

Alex Doherty

Erin Gettis, Assoc. AIA

John Henderson, FAIA

Romero Hernandez

Anne Hewitt and
David Garrison

Paul Joelson, AIA

Bethany Johnson,
Assoc. AIA

Mario Lara

Jeanne McCallum, AIA

Gregory Mellberg, AIA

Ben Meza, AIA

Robert Mosher, FAIA

Eric Naslund, AIA

Patrick O'Donnell,
Assoc. AIA

Hector Reyes, AIA

Phillip Scholtz Rittermann

San Diego Historical Society
Photograph Collection

Ernesto Santos, Assoc. AIA

Diana Scheffler

Jerry Shonkwiler, AIA

James Skovmand:
San Diego Union-Tribune

Tom Stepat

Dirk Sutro

El Colegio de Arquitectos
de Tijuana

University of California
San Diego

Xan Waldron

Brian Washburn

Reviewing Team

Harold Sadler, FAIA

John Henderson, FAIA

Michael Stepner, FAIA

Members of SOHO

Catharine Herbst, AIA

Dr. Ray Brandeis

Donna Alm, APR

Garry Papers, AIA

Research Team

John Henderson, FAIA

Brian Washburn

Monique Parsons

Christine Alexander

Students of The NewSchool
of Architecture and Design

Maria E. Castillo Curry

Mapping Team

Kevin Carpenter,
Assoc. AIA,
Mapping Chair

Todd Carpenter

Kurt Wittkow

Omneya Salem

Ernesto Santos, Assoc. AIA

Monica Lopez

George Campos

ACKNOWLEDGEMENTS

Transit Maps

Courtesy of
Metropolitan Transit
Development Board (MTDB)

Distribution

Distributed by
Sunbelt Publications

Printing

Printed by Rush Press

101 Market Street 44

202 Island Inn 44

235 on Market 44

600 Front Street 43

A

Aerospace Museum 109

Albright, Harrison 30, 31, 46, 51, 66, 108

Alcazar Garden 106

Allen, Frank P. 67, 92, 106

Allen, Stephen 37

Altamirano-Pedrorena House 116

American Institute of Architects, San Diego Chapter 9

Amici Park 86

ARC Design International 44

Architects|Larson|Carpenter 103

ARK Architects 82

Arlington Hotel 68

Armed Services YMCA 29

Armitage & Wilson 56

Asian-Pacific Historic District 53

Austin Hansen Design Group 53

Austin Hansen Fehlman 43

Austin Veum Robbins Partners 122, 124

Avion 122

Aztec Theatre/Urban Outfitters 56

B

Backesto Building 55

Bakewell & Brown 28

Balboa Park 90

Balboa Park Activity Center 109

Balboa Theatre 50

Beaumont Building 85

Beckett, Welton 40

Bella Via 83

Benson Bohl Architects 121

Botanical Building + Lily Pond 104

Bridgeworks 52

Brisebois, Robin 83

Bristow and Lyman 61

Broadway Manor 67

Brunswig Drug Company 54

Bundy & Thompson 32, 102, 125

Burkett & Osgood 55

Burnham, Daniel 92

Burnham, Franklin P. 33

C

Cabrillo Bridge 106

Cabrillo, Juan 14

California Building/Museum of Man 105

California Stamp Building 82

California Theatre 36

Camden Tuscany 82

Carrier Johnson 28, 29, 43, 51, 52, 83

Casa de Balboa 103

Casa de Bandini 116

Casa de Estudillo 116

Casa de Machado y Silva 115

Casa de Machado y Stewart 115

Casa Del Prado 103

Centre City Development Corp. 6, 9, 12

Children's Museum, (New San Diego) 125

Children's Museum Park 125

Christian Science Church 36

City Front Terrace 40

City Walk 42

CityMark on Cortez Hill 74

Clement & Stannard 52, 59

Coast Hotel/Occidental Hotel 68

Cole Block Building 57

Coliseum Athletic Club/Jerome's Furniture Warehouse 67

Colorado House/ Wells Fargo History Museum 115

Comstock & Trotsche 46, 59, 69

Coronado Bridge 37

Cortez Hill 70

Cortez Hill Park/Tweet Street 75

Cortez Hill Transitional Housing 74

County Administration Center 87

Crabtree Building 36

Crown Bay 45

Curtiss, Glenn 17

Cunningham, Wallace 3

D

Dalton Building 61

Dana, Richard Henry 14, 111

David Baker Architects 121

Davids Killory 7

Davis, William Heath 15

Day, Clinton 56

Decker, Clarence 34

Deems Lewis 5, 22, 40

Deems-Martin 36

DeFalco's Grocery/San Diego Reader 86

Delawie, Homer 5

Delawie Bretton Wilkes 69

Derby-Pendleton House 117

Diamond Terrace 121

Dikeakos and Cotter 41

Discovery at Cortez Hill 75

Doma Lofts and Towns 82

Dominy & Associates 8

Donaldson, Milford Wayne 28, 52, 54, 98

Downtown 12

Dr. W. Peper Residence 76

E

Eagles Hall 68

Earp, Wyatt 59

East Village 62

East West Building 54

El Cortez Hotel 14, 70, 75

Entrada Apartments 122

Essex Lofts 88

Eugene Hoffman & Andrew Ervast 28

Exposition of 1935 95

F

Federal Building & U.S. Courthouse 30

Fehlman LaBarre 45, 121

Filippi's Pizza Grotto/ Albert Muller Grocery 88

Fire Station #4 69

Fire Station/Museum 84

First National Bank Building 33

First National Bank Tower 35

First San Diego Courthouse 115

Fletcher-Lovett Building 66

Ford Building/Aerospace Museum 109

Ford/Starlight Bowl 108

Fritz Building 57

G

Gaslamp Liquor/Lawton's Car Hop Restaurant 68

Gaslamp Pacific Stadium 15 57

Gaslamp Quarter 46

Gaslamp Quarter Park 53

Gay, Henry Lord 77

George Hill Building 58

Gianninni & Ferguson 85

Gill, Irving 3, 4, 23, 31, 111

Gill, Louis 53, 68, 87

Gluckman Mayner 28

Golba Architecture 74

Golden West Hotel 51

Goodhue, Bertram 5, 17, 19, 87, 92, 93, 94, 96, 98, 105, 109

Goodrich, Levi 55

Grand Pacific Hotel 52

The Grande At Santa Fe Place 124

Granger Building 31

Gray, Andrew 15

Grondona, Tom 5

H

Hall of Justice 29

Hamill, Sam 87

Hampton Inn 84

Hanssen, Gustav A. 69

Hearne Surgical Hospital 77

Hebbard, William 67

Hebbard & Gill 36, 76

Heritage Apartments 75

Heritage Park Victorian Village 117

Hoffman, Eugene 52

Hornberger & Worstell 123

Hope, Frank L. 40, 104

Hope & Wheeler 30

Hope Architects 41

Horizons 44

Horton, Alonzo 14, 90

Horton Grand/Kahle Saddlery Hotels 52

Horton on Fourth Apartments 51

Horton Plaza 32

Horton Plaza Park and Fountain 31

Hotel Mediterranean 67

House of Charm 106

House of Hospitality 107

House of Pacific Relations 108

Hyatt Regency San Diego 40

Hyndman & Hyndman 8

I

I.O.O.F. Building 55

Imperial Bank 35

India Street Design Center/ San Diego Coffee Co. 89

IIngersoll Tutton Building 60

Ingle Building/Golden Lion 50

Interstate 5 78

J

Jahn, Helmut 22

J Street Inn 45

Japanese Friendship Garden 108

Jenkins, Dale 103

Jerde, Jon 12, 22, 32

Jerde Partnership 32

John D. Spreckels Building 34

Johnson, William Templeton 5, 20, 28, 34, 66, 87, 102, 104, 111, 114

K

William Kettner 18

Keating Building 60

Kelley-Markham, Jim 74

Kennedy, S.G. 67

C.W. Kim 29

Klauber-Wangenheim Building 68

Julius Kraft & Sons 69

L

La Pensione 86

Lacy, William 56, 58

Langdon & Wilson 35

Lawyer's Block Building 50

Lester Hotel 51

Light-Freeman House 114

LIND 83

Little Italy 78

Llewelyn Building 57

Lofts at 777 Sixth Avenue 121

Loring Building 57

Louis Bank of Commerce 59

Lusso Lofts 83

M

M2i 122

Main Library 122

Withee Malcolm 44, 45, 85

Marsh, Norman 66

Marston Building 59

Martin Luther King, Jr. Promenade 13, 22, 43

Martinez + Cutri Corporation 40, 42, 82, 84, 122

Marum, Marian 86

Maryland Hotel 67

Mason Street School 115

McDonough Cleaners/City Dye Works 82

McDougall and Sons 50

McGurck Building/Z Gallerie 55

McKinley & Associates 74

Mead, Frank 111

Medical/Dental Building 36

Metropolitan Correctional Center 42

Mills Building 69

Mills Residence 76

Milton E. Fintzelberg Commercial Building 88

Mimmo's Italian Village/Auto Body Company 87

Mingei Museum 106

Moore, Charles 8

Mosher, Robert 37

Municipal Gym 108

Murphy/Jahn 29

M.W. Steele Group 76

N

Natural History Museum 102

Naval Hospital 109

Nesmith-Greeley Building 59

Nestor and Gaffney 42

New San Diego Children's Museum 125

New School of Architecture 62

Ninth and Beech 74

Ninth and Broadway 125

Nolen, John 6, 70

North Embarcadero Alliance Visionary Plan 23

O

Old Adobe Chapel 117

Old City Hall 56

Old Globe Theatre 105

Old Main Post Office 66

Old Town 14, 110

Olmsted 90, 92, 93

Omni Hotel 123

On Broadway 32

One America Plaza 29

Onyx Building 61

Our Lady of the Rosary Church and Parish Hall 85

P

Pacific Terrace 45

Palms Hotel 69

Panama-California Exposition 70

Pantoja Park 41

PAPA 51

Park Blvd. Revitalization 123

Park Place 41

Parkinson & Parkinson 34

Parsons, Samuel Jr. 90

John Perkins & Co. 75, 120

John Paxton Perrine 36

Perkins & Company 124

Petco Park 123

Pickwick Hotel/Greyhound Bus Terminal 30

Pierrot Theatre/First Baptist Church 66

Pinnacle Museum Tower 124

Pioneer Warehouse Lofts 52

Porto Siena 85

Predock, Antoine 6

Public 83

Q

Quayle, William 31, 51

Quayle, Edward 50

Quayle Brothers 41, 77

Quigley, Rob 3, 5, 7, 12, 43, 44, 45, 55, 79, 83, 85, 86, 99, 109, 122, 125

R

Reid brothers 60

Renaissance 43

Requa, Richard 5, 87, 95, 96, 98, 102, 107, 108, 111

Requa & Jackson 37

Reuben H. Fleet Science Center 109

Rice, David 103

Riviera Apartments 66

RNP 54

Roberto Martinez/Sheldon Residence 69

Rodgers, Lincoln 29

Royal Pie Bakery 51

Ruocco, Lloyd 3, 5, 103

S

The San Diego Architectural Foundation 9

Samuel I. Fox Building 34

San Diego Athletic Club/HBJ Building/World Trade Center 35

San Diego City College 62

San Diego Convention and Visitors Bureau 9

San Diego Convention Center 40

San Diego Globe Grain & Milling Co./ Parron-Hall 84

San Diego Hardware 60

San Diego Historical Society 9

San Diego Macaroni Manufacturing Co. 82

San Diego Marriott Hotel 40

San Diego Museum of Art 104

San Diego Police Headquarters 41

San Diego Trolley 12, 47, 63

San Diego Trust & Savings 34

San Diego Union Museum 116

San Diego Zoo 103

Sanford Hotel 77

Santa Fe Depot Baggage Building 28

Sasaki Associates 23

Schmidt, Max 22

Schwartz, Martha 43

SDG&E Station B 28

SDG&E Substation C/ Consolidated Gas & Electric Company 37

Seaport Village 41

Security Pacific Plaza 36

Seely Stables 116

Segal, Jonathan 12, 41, 79, 82, 83

Serra Museum 114

Sessions, Kate 90

Seven on Kettner 41

Sferra-Carnini 85

Siebert, John S. 67, 68

Silvas-McCoy House 114

Skidmore Owings & Merrill 22, 35, 40

Smith, Ted 3, 5, 79

Smith & Others 74, 83, 88

Soleil Court 74

Solomon Cordwell & Buenz 40

Spanish Village 102

Spencer Ogden/DeLaval Building 58

Spreckels Organ Pavilion 108

Spreckels Theatre 30

Spurlock Poirier 125

St. Cecilia Chapel 76

St. James Hotel 58

Standard Sanitary Manufacturing Company 84

Star of India 45

Starkman, Maxwell 42

Starlight Bowl 108

Stevenson, Frank 36

Stevenson, F.W. 29, 34, 35, 61

Stewart Brothers 59

Studio E 7, 122

Symphony Towers 35

T

T.R. Produce Warehouse/ Wellman Peck and Company 69

Taylor, James Knox 42

Temporary Paradise 7

The Baltic Inn 55

The Buckner 67

The Meridian 42

The Mills at Cortez Hill 76

Timken Building 66

Timken Museum 104

Tochey, Jaime 30

Togawa & Smith 75

Treganza, A.O. 41

Treo at Kettner 28

Tucker Sadler & Bennett 35, 36, 103

Tucker-Sadler 5, 22, 35, 40, 42

Tucker Sadler Noble Castro 122

U

U.S. Custom and Courthouse 42

U.S. Grant Hotel 31

Union Bank 35

V

Veitzer, Leonard 5

Victorian House Condominiums 85

Village Walk 84

Vue de L'Eau Apartments 88

W

Walker, Peter 43

Walker and Eisen 21, 70, 75

Ware & Malcolm 35

Waterfront Apartments 82

Watts-Robinson Building/ Jewelers Exchange 61

Whaley House Museum 117

Wheeler, William 35, 50, 68

William Heath Davis House 54

Wheeler Wimer 103

Wimmer-Yamada Building 54

Carleton Winslow 104, 107

Wong, Joseph 84

Woodbury University 62

Wright, Frank Lloyd 4, 46

Wright, John Lloyd 51

Wrightington House 114

Wyndham Emerald Plaza 29

Y

Yuma Building 56

YWCA 34

Z

Zimmer & Reamer 58